WHITE WINGS

SCENE FROM ACT I

WHITE WINGS

A PLAY BY

PHILIP BARRY

With an Introduction by
DONALD OGDEN STEWART

1 9 2 7

BONI & LIVERIGHT · NEW YORK

N O T E

INTRODUCTION

THE GROWING INFLUENCE OF THE STREET CLEANER IN MODERN AMERICAN DRAMA *

By Donald Ogden Stewart

Mr. Stewart: Young ladies of the Junior League of Hartford and friends—

The Chairman: But Mr. Stewart—this isn't the Junior League of Hartford—

Mr. Stewart: No?

The Chairman: No.

Mr. Stewart: What is to-day?

The Chairman [*consulting a calendar*]: July 4th, 1926.

Mr. Stewart [*obviously embarrassed*]: My mistake.

[*A pause.*]

* From an address delivered by Mr. Stewart before the Annual Convention of the Ellsworth Society at Atlantic City on July 4, 1926.

THE CHAIRMAN: Will you open that window, please, Miss Gillespie.

[*Another pause.*]

MR. STEWART [*a little doubtfully*]: Young ladies of the Ellsworth Society—

THE CHAIRMAN: That's right, Mr. Stewart.

MR. STEWART: —and friends. I am very happy to be with you to-day. I am particularly happy because I have just finished reading a wonderful play —a play in which I am sure you will all be very much interested.

THE CHAIRMAN: The other window, too, Miss Gillespie. Thank you.

MR. STEWART: As you all know, there have been hundreds of plays about Street Cleaners—plays in which the Street Cleaner was the hero—plays in which he was the villain—plays in which he was merely the atmosphere or an off-stage noise. [*Laughter.*]

THE CHAIRMAN: Young ladies—please!

MR. STEWART: But the main objection—or one of the main objections—to all of those earlier attempts to depict the life of the White Wing in terms of tragic beauty or heroic comedy was the fact that in every case the author of the play had not himself been a Street Cleaner and did not, on that account (to quote the Bible), "speak with authority." [*Laughter.*]

THE CHAIRMAN: "Speak *as one in* authority," I believe, Mr. Stewart.

MR. STEWART: Thank you. In fact, he spoke "as in a glass darkly," and his truths were too often apt to resemble the story about the death of Mark Twain which, as you remember, was "greatly exaggerated."

THE CHAIRMAN: I knew Twain very well.

MR. STEWART: And so it is with a great deal of pleasure that I can report to you this afternoon that Philip Barry, the author of this play that I am going to recommend to you, was for a brief period employed by the Department of Street Cleaning—and thereby hangs a tale.

THE CHAIRMAN [*to the lady directly behind him*]: I knew Twain very well.

MR. STEWART: I had met Barry when he was an undergraduate at Yale and I had heard that at college he was more or less interested in literature and the drama—even to the extent of wanting to write poetry and plays himself. I did not see him for some time after that and I naturally supposed that after graduation he had gone in for advertising or the bond business.

THE CHAIRMAN: Eleven minutes, Mr. Stewart.

MR. STEWART: But I fear that my time is growing short.

THE CHAIRMAN: Yes.

MR. STEWART: Well, to make a long story short (applause)—one morning—or perhaps it was two or three months ago—I was coming out of the Yale Club and as I turned the corner into 44th Street—or perhaps it was 45th Street—

THE CHAIRMAN: Thirteen minutes, Mr. Stewart.

MR. STEWART: Well, to make a long story short (laughter)—I saw a Street Cleaner pushing his broom along and when I came closer I realized, with somewhat of a shock, that it was either Philip Barry or some one who looked an awful lot like him.

"Pardon me," I said, stepping out into the street, "but either you are Philip Barry or some one who looks an awful lot like him."

THE CHAIRMAN: Miss Gillespie, I'm afraid that you will have to ask the janitor to let us have the electric lights now.

MR. STEWART: Well, in that particular case it turned out that the Street Cleaner was *not* Philip Barry but a man named Hobson—Raymond Hobson—and so I went on down the street. But it set me thinking that a very original play could be written about Street Cleaners and so, when I heard that Philip Barry had written just that kind of a play, I made haste to get it and read it. I wish that every one of you would do the same. I wish that every one of you could see what a fine piece of work Mr. Barry has done. I had hoped to be able to read at least part of this play to you this afternoon. But I am afraid that my time is almost up—

THE CHAIRMAN: To put it mildly, Mr. Stewart.

Mr. Stewart: And so I will simply close by thanking you very much and by hoping that when you do read Mr. Barry's play you will enjoy it one half as much as I did.

The Chairman: That concludes the program for to-day.

To

DONALD OGDEN STEWART

"Are you fond of horses?" asked Mrs. Haddock sympathetically.

"I detest horses," said Mr. Perkins with a sudden convulsive grasp of his broom handle.

"Oh," said Mrs. Haddock, biting her lip, "I'm so sorry. I forgot."

—*Mr. and Mrs. Haddock Abroad.*

CAST OF FIRST PRODUCTION

"WHITE WINGS" was first produced by Winthrop Ames at the Booth Theater, New York City, on October 15, 1926. It was directed by Winthrop Ames, the settings were designed by Woodman Thompson, and the cast was as follows:

JOSEPH, *a Horse*............George Ali
MARY TODD...............Winifred Lenihan
ARCHIE INCH..............Tom Powers
MR. ERNEST INCH..........William Norris
HERBERT, *a Cabby*.........J. M. Kerrigan
PAUL PILLSBURY ⎫ *White* ⎧ Donald McKee
RALPH OTIS   ⎬ *Wings* ⎨ Earl McDonald
CLYDE SIMS, III ⎭   ⎩ Ben Lackland
KIT CANARI................Donald Macdonald
MRS. FANNY K. INCH........Jessie Graham
MAJOR PHILIP E. INCH......Albert Tavernier
CHARLIE TODD ....Arthur Allen
DR. BOWLES ....Donald McKee
DR. DERBY ....Earl McDonald
TAXI-DRIVER ....Ben Lackland
CITY EMPLOYEE ....Phil Sheridan

CHARACTERS

MAJOR PHILIP E. INCH

MR. ERNEST INCH

MRS. FANNY K. INCH

ARCHIE INCH

CHARLIE TODD

MARY TODD

KIT CANARI

PAUL PILLSBURY ⎫
RALPH OTIS ⎬ *White Wings*
CLYDE SIMS, III ⎭

HERBERT, *a Cabby*

DR. BOWLES

DR. DERBY

A TAXI-DRIVER

A CITY EMPLOYEE

JOSEPH, *a Horse*

ACTION AND SCENE

The action of the play takes place in the streets of an American city at varying intervals between 1895 and 1915.

Act I

The Boulevard

Act II

Scene 1—The Parkway
Scene 2—The Parkway

Act III

The Parkway

NOTE: The settings for the three acts should be so designed as to key the action of the play just out of reality. This may be accomplished by means of a realistic foreground and backgrounds painted "in the flat" to give a poster-effect.

WHITE WINGS : ACT ONE

ACT I

A section of the Boulevard, backed by a long wall which supports the Parkway. This wall must be low enough to show, in the setting for Act Two (which is the reverse of this setting), the head and shoulders of the Cabby, who sits upon the box of his cab in the Boulevard.

On the wall, obliterating part of a "Post No Bills" sign, are several of the advertising posters of the period. Among them "Doctor Munyon" with his finger upraised and his reassuring "There is Hope."

A narrow, curbed sidewalk runs along the back wall and follows the line of a two-storied brick building, which juts out at Right. At the angle of the wall a brief flight of stone steps leads up to the Parkway. Above the main entrance to the building is a sign "The Elite. Sea Food. Family Entrance," the mica-surface of which is illuminated by a Welsbach-burner enclosed in a glass globe. Below it the picture of a goat's head simply announces "Bock." The second story of

17

the building (which rises above the Parkway wall) is seen to be brightly lighted, although the window-blinds are drawn. From off left, a gas street-light adds a little more illumination to the scene. There is a moon in the sky and a mass of clouds framing it. Dimly in the background past the Parkway the outlines of a few buildings may be seen.

Backed against the curbstone beside the restaurant stands an old-fashioned open cab. The cabby is absent from the box, and the absurd figure of a horse, his sides bulging, is nodding in his traces. He is held by an iron weight, fastened to his bit, and wears a bunch of leaves over one ear. This is JOSEPH, and there are two men in him.

The time is about two o'clock on a spring morning in the late Nineties.

At rise, piano and violin music is heard from the upper story of the restaurant. The horse flips an ear, turns his head and listens for the music. Nods again, then turns his head toward the wall, listens. Then shakes his head, lets himself down upon the pavement, and goes to sleep.

The door of the restaurant is opened, and MARY TODD *comes out, on the arm of* ARCHIE

Inch, *who is a nice-looking boy of about twenty.*
Mary *is eighteen, gay, pretty, attractive. She
carries a stiff little bouquet of flowers.* Archie,
in white duck trousers and short blue coat, and
Mary, *in a party-dress, with a broad sash and a
ribbon at the back of her hair, are dressed in the
fashion of the period. In the middle of the street*
Mary *stops, takes her arm from* Archie's, *and
goes back to the step of the restaurant.*

ARCHIE

What's the matter?

MARY

My slipper—I've got to fix it.
    [*She takes it off, fusses at the heel and replaces
        it.*]

ARCHIE

I suppose it'll go on all night.

MARY

It'll—?   What'll—?
    [Archie *glances toward the lighted windows.*]

ARCHIE

—That'll—[*The music stops.   He explains.*]
—Kit's party.   [Mary *yawns.*]

MARY

It was fun, wasn't it?

ARCHIE

[*Gallantly.*]
I met *you*, Miss Todd.

MARY

Still—it was fun. . . . [*A moment, then she starts toward left.*] But gracious—when I saw that clock!

ARCHIE

Where are you going?

MARY

Home, of course.
   [*He offers his arm. She takes it. They smile at each other.*]

ARCHIE

Where's "home"?

MARY

Poplar Street.

ARCHIE

[*Indicating the cab.*]
Let's take this.
   [*Mary laughs.*]

MARY

Six blocks? Don't be silly.

ARCHIE

[*Shyly.*]

It's—always been a—sort of an ambition of mine to take a girl home in a cab—a—an *open* cab.

[*She stares at him. He smiles engagingly.*]
You'd—I'd appreciate it ever so much, if you would.

MARY

But there's no one to— [*The horse drags himself to his feet.*] Please don't get up. [*To* ARCHIE.]
But there's no one to drive the beast.

ARCHIE

[*Eagerly.*]

I know the cabby. He's a friend of mine. He's probably just stepped into a saloon. *I* can find him.

[MARY *eyes the horse distrustfully.*]

MARY

—And leave me alone with that monster? Not on your life.

—Have you got a watch?

ARCHIE

Yes.

MARY

We'll wait ten minutes for the cabby to come. Then we'll walk. [*She seats herself upon a beer-box against the restaurant wall.*] Um—this is pleasant. I like gutters. I was practically raised in one. We'll wait eleven minutes. Here— [*She indicates a place upon another box at her side.* ARCHIE *looks at the horse, and hesitates.*] What's the matter?

ARCHIE

I suppose it's kind of foolish, but I never like to sit while a horse is standing. Sort of—you know— sign of respect.

    [MARY *laughs delightedly. The horse gestures graciously for* ARCHIE *to sit down.*]

MARY

You're a great jollier, aren't you?

ARCHIE

"Jollier"—?

    [*He seats himself beside* MARY.]

MARY

I've never been out this late. I hope sleep finally overcomes Father.

    [*The horse settles himself again and goes to sleep.*]

ARCHIE

My father's always up late. Mother says he's a prowler.

MARY

A what?

ARCHIE

A night-prowler. Even after being on duty all day long, he'll prowl the streets till nearly morning. It's as if he was looking for something—something he'd lost.

MARY

Poor man.

ARCHIE

I don't think he's very happy.

MARY

Mine's terribly happy. He's a mechanical genius. I am, too, in a smaller way. I don't suppose I ought to tell you, but we're going to revolutionize the world.

ARCHIE

When, especially?

MARY

To-morrow afternoon. [ARCHIE *laughs*.] You can laugh!— But just you stand around the streets a little to-morrow.

ARCHIE

That's my job— Any street in particular?

MARY

Up there on the Parkway. You'll see history made to-morrow.

ARCHIE

That ought to be— [*He yawns.*] —More fun than reading it.

> [MARY *yawns also. The piano and violin begin another tune.*]

MARY

You sleepy, too?

ARCHIE

I am, a little.

MARY

All of a sudden.

ARCHIE

Um.

MARY

Rather pleasant sensation.

ARCHIE

'Tis, isn't it?

SCENE FROM ACT I

MARY

Like—being—just a little bit drunk, I suppose.

ARCHIE

I don't know.

MARY

I feel it first in the back of my neck. Sleep, I mean.

ARCHIE

It's awfully pretty.

MARY

What is?

ARCHIE

The back of your neck.

MARY

Is it? I've never seen it. [*A pause.*] It's my ears, *I* like. Look— [*She raises her hand to brush the hair back from an ear, but is too sleepy to complete the motion and lets it fall again.*] —Some other time.

ARCHIE

I'll bet they're peacherinos— Don't forget.

MARY

Remind me— [*They begin to breathe regularly, in unison.* MARY *leans against him.*] Funny—even with my eyes shut, I can see your face. [*Another pause.*] —It's a funny face, even for a man. *I* like it. And I like the way you sit down— You sit down with a will.

ARCHIE

I try to do everything that way.

MARY

It must be a strain at times.

ARCHIE

I've got the constitution of the United States.

MARY

Some day you must tell me all about it.

ARCHIE

To-morrow—may I call?

MARY

I'll be too tired. I told you I've got the world to revolutionize.

ARCHIE

The day after?

MARY

I promised to pitch quoits with friends.

ARCHIE

Thursday.

MARY

My Sunday-school class meets Thursday. [*A pause. In a far-away voice.*] Oh—I'm going under. I'm slipping—slipping. It's—ver' pleasant—verrr' pleas-ant— [*Faintly.*] Cabby! Cabby!

> [*A long pause. Their breathing becomes more and more regular. The music stops. Gradually MARY's head sinks down upon his shoulder and his arm goes about her, as she settles against him. His other hand gropes for hers and finds it. He bends his head and rests his cheek against her brow. Then, prowling furtively along from Left, the Parkway above them, comes the figure of a sad, nervous little man of about forty, in a white-duck uniform and white helmet. This is MR. ERNEST INCH. He stops at a point directly above them, leans on his arms upon the wall and sadly contemplates the space before his eyes.*]

MR. INCH

[*Softly.*]

Where's it gone to—my pretty life? Oh, what's become of it? [*A pause. Then he glances down and sees* ARCHIE *and* MARY. *He looks closely at* ARCHIE, *fumbles for his watch, brings it forth, examines it, returns it to his pocket, leans over the wall and whispers.*] Archie! [*There is no response.* ARCHIE *glances upwards, then shuts his eyes tighter.*] Son! [*Still no response. He waits an instant and whispers a little louder.*] Archie! Go home to bed.

[*Again no response. Then, after a moment,* MARY *speaks, as if from a dream.*]

MARY

"Archie," did you say your name was?

ARCHIE

Archie.
[MR. INCH *leans back from the wall and cups his chin thoughtfully in his hand.*]

MARY

Darling Archie. . . .

ARCHIE

[*Rousing himself.*]
What—? What's that you say?
[*The horse wakes up.*]

MARY

Never mind. Let's sleep awhile. Darling . . . darling. . . .

ARCHIE

I heard you that time! Listen! There's something I want to ask you—

MARY

Shhh! Later. Go to sleep, now. . . . [*For a long time they do not speak.* MR. INCH *stands regarding them with a troubled expression, biting his nails.* ARCHIE'S *arm brings* MARY *closer and closer to him. Except for this barely perceptible motion, they might be asleep. The horse cocks his head in their direction, and begins to roll his eyes savagely from them to* MR. INCH. MR. INCH *nervously gestures to the horse to be quiet, and the horse becomes quieter.* ARCHIE *slowly bends his head and kisses* MARY *upon the cheek. After an instant she averts her face murmuring:*] Ah—that was nice. . . . [*Again* ARCHIE'S *arm tightens about her, and this time she lifts her face to his.* MR. INCH *is gazing at them, spellbound.* ARCHIE *is about to kiss* MARY *for the second time, when suddenly the horse whinnies sharply.* MARY *starts, in alarm.* MR. INCH *covers his eyes with his hand, and goes off, Right.* MARY *grasps* ARCHIE'S *arm and looks fearfully behind her.*] What was it?

ARCHIE

Just the horse. [*The horse begins to paw the ground.*] He must have heard something. They hear things we don't. [*Unseen by* ARCHIE, MARY *makes a threatening gesture toward the animal.* ARCHIE'S *face is shining with joy.*] Darling—isn't it wonderful?

MARY

Oh, I don't know. Dogs smell things we don't.

ARCHIE

I mean—that we *love* each other.

MARY

[*Aghast.*]
That we *what* each other?

ARCHIE

[*Happily.*]
Love!

MARY

Well, for jumping to conclusions.

ARCHIE

What's your name? Your whole name?

MARY

Mary Todd. But—
[ARCHIE *repeats the name, as if tasting it.*]

ARCHIE

"Mary Todd." I like that— We must be married soon— When shall we be married, Mary?

MARY

How would, say, nineteen-ten or twenty do?

ARCHIE

Don't joke.

MARY

[*Indulgently.*]
Now, listen, child—

ARCHIE

We're engaged to be married!

MARY

[*Gently.*]
—And you wanted me to be the first to know. I do appreciate that. [ARCHIE *turns from her, miserably. She laughs.*] So just because two people want to kiss each other, they get married!

[ARCHIE's *honest eyes meet hers again without wavering.*]

ARCHIE

They'll never find a better reason.

MARY

Of all the— [*Suddenly she becomes grave.*] You know, that sounds quite wise.

ARCHIE

It *is* quite wise.

MARY

You're a funny boy.

ARCHIE

I love *you*, Mary.

MARY

To-morrow you won't.

ARCHIE

To-morrow ten years, I shall. I'm as funny as that.

[MARY *ponders.*]

MARY

You *are* nice. And I *would* like to get married some day to a really *nic*e man. [*A pause. Then, suddenly.*] Listen—do you like engines?

ARCHIE

I'm afraid not. What have engines got to do with—

MARY

You don't know anything about them! I know everything about them! They're the most thrilling, exciting—

ARCHIE

I'm afraid I wouldn't care for them. It's horses I like. I love horses.

[MARY *regards him for a moment quizzically.*]

MARY

—In fact you worship the ground they walk on.

ARCHIE

Well—yes—in a way.

MARY

And in addition to worshipping it, you sweep it.

ARCHIE

That's—a form of worship, I suppose.

MARY

You *are* a great jollier, aren't you?

ARCHIE

Why?

MARY

—Telling me you're a street-cleaner, and all
that—

ARCHIE

[*With dignity.*]
—A White Wing, if you please.

MARY

Well then, a White Wing.

ARCHIE

'Tisn't very surprising, is it?— We Inches have
been White Wings for generations.
[MARY *turns quickly and grasps his arm.*]

MARY

Your name isn't Inch?

ARCHIE

Yes, it is. "Archibald Inch." My friends call
me "Archie."

MARY

"A-A-Archie Inch"—

ARCHIE

[*Pleased.*]
That's right.

—But "Mary Todd"! Think!—"Todd." [*He looks at her wonderingly.*] My father's name's Charlie Todd.— Remember?

ARCHIE

I know a Charles Doremus—that wouldn't be him?

MARY

No, no! Father used to be your furnace man— years ago— [ARCHIE *frowns.*] —Your Mother discharged him on account of the engines he kept building in the cellar. They used to smell a little. He told me all about you once—remember your seventh birthday?

ARCHIE

I don't remember anything that happened before I was ten.

[MARY *gazes at him intently.*]

MARY

—He said that you— [*She stops abruptly, then concludes.*] —Well, something must have changed you. I don't see how you could have grown into this, from that. —Have you been a White Wing long?

ARCHIE

[*With pride.*]
Two years.

MARY

—But aren't you awfully young?

ARCHIE

I'm over twenty.

MARY

Dear me.

ARCHIE

I'm Chief of one of the Boulevard divisions. My cart's up there— [*He points over his shoulder to the Parkway.*] On a clear day you can see it from here. [*He ponders.*] "Charlie Todd"— [*And shakes his head.*] Nope.

MARY

He's practically the greatest man in the world.

ARCHIE

I admire greatness. Amongst us Inches it is a family tradition to be content with nothing short of genuine public achievement. Do you know anything about horses?

[MR. INCH *reënters from Right on the Parkway, stops and listens.*]

MARY

Only the usual gossip, I'm afraid.

ARCHIE

[*Obviously quoting some one.*]

I hope you appreciate the important part Horse has played in the advance of Civilization. From an obscure beginning in the army and upon the farm, he has gradually become the very axis about which our social and economic life revolves.

MARY

You don't say.

ARCHIE

Yes, I do. —And directly, Mary—directly upon the heels of generations of horses, have come generations of Inches.

MARY

Good for them—

ARCHIE

—Of course the *first* Inches came over on the *Mayflower*—

MARY

But the horses—they were here already.

ARCHIE

Yes.

MARY

Father says *our* ancestors ran for the *Mayflower*
and missed it.

ARCHIE

Look—here's a tintype of us taken in uniform
last summer at the Lake. See?— Three generations of White Wings.

MARY

The second one must have moved.

ARCHIE

That's Papa. Cameras make him nervous. Anything that clicks suddenly.

[Mr. Inch *begins to bite his nails.*]

MARY

I'll bet nothing scares Grandpa. Is he as fierce
as his whiskers?

ARCHIE

He more or less founded the family.

MARY

I can easily believe it.

ARCHIE

For the second time, that is. *Re*-founded it, you might say. Yes, even after the final failure of the Inch-by-Inch Community Idea in '63—even then the old Inch Idealism still burned true. Grandfather— but probably you've heard of *him*, in connection with General Boocock's march upon Antietam.

MARY

I'm a little weak on the Civil War.

ARCHIE

For the fact that a thousand horse rode two hundred miles without leaving a single clue, one man was responsible. And that man was my grandfather—Major Philip Inch—at that time Corporal Inch.

MARY

I like Papa best. He looks sweet.
[Mr. Inch *smiles faintly*.]

ARCHIE

It's a pity he's so unhappy.
[*The smile leaves* Mr. Inch's *face*.]

MARY

Is he always?
[Archie *nods*.]

ARCHIE

I don't know why, exactly. Maybe it's because—
Well—you see, they had hoped for a large family,
but I'm an only child, Mary. I'm the last of our
line.

MARY

But that's not *his* fault!
[MR. INCH's *lip begins to quiver.*]

ARCHIE

No, maybe not. [MR. INCH *rests his head upon
his arms and begins to cry softly over the wall.*]
Still, he's inclined to take things personally—so
we've made it a rule never to mention big families
in his presence.

MARY

That's considerate, I'm sure.

ARCHIE

It avoids scenes. I hate scenes.

MARY

Do you like olives?

ARCHIE

Olives?—

MARY

I just thought I'd change the subject. [*One of* MR. INCH's *tears splashes down upon her hand.*] Why! It's raining.

[MR. INCH *fades into the background and goes out, Right.*]

ARCHIE

No, it's not.

MARY

I felt a drop on my hand. Look— [ARCHIE *examines her hand, then gazes, puzzled, into the air. A little river of tears is now running down the Parkway wall. They rise and look at it.*] It's certainly raining up there. See there!

ARCHIE

Maybe we're just on the edge of a storm.

MARY

I wish friend cabby would come.

ARCHIE

He will.

[*She looks at him closely.*]

MARY

—A White Wing. [*Then, with decision.*] Never mind—I like you anyway.

ARCHIE

[*Puzzled.*]

—"Anyway"—?

[*She nods, then raises her finger hopefully, in
imitation of the finger of "Dr. Munyon" in
the poster.*]

MARY

Look, Archie; Doctor Munyon: "There is hope!"
I can save you!   Come with my father and me;
we've put the cart before the horse.

ARCHIE

You've done what?

MARY

Literally—cart before the horse.   In fact, no
horse whatever.   We've dispensed with him.

ARCHIE

You know, I can't make you out at all.

[MARY *gazes for a moment full into his eyes.
Then she picks up one of his hands, looks at
it intently, lifts it to her lips, kisses it, and
drops it again.*]

MARY

Nor can I you.

ARCHIE

[*Lowly.*]
Why did you do that?

MARY

—Dunno. I never know why I do things. I just do them.

[*She walks away from him toward the horse.*]

ARCHIE

I've never known a girl like you. I've never even imagined one.

[MARY *laughs.*]

MARY

Maybe I'm something new. I am!— A speed-engine on wheels! You—you're just a handsome horse, with winning ways. [*The horse stamps.*] Everything about you's as back-number as— [*She eyes the horse.*] —As your fat friend here will be when Dad and I get through with him. [*She pulls a face at the animal.*] Oh, you don't know what's coming to *you*, my Black Beauty! [*Suddenly the horse bares his teeth and makes a lunge at her. She ducks, then turns angrily and gives him a sharp blow upon the nose with her fist.*] Get away, you fool! [*She examines her knuckles.*] Well, of all the nerve.

ARCHIE

[*Advancing.*]
You dare hit that horse!

MARY

Did you see what he did? [*To the horse.*]
—Know your natural enemy, don't you? Well,
here's one for Father—

[*She squares off again.* ARCHIE *leaps between
her and the horse.*]

ARCHIE

Stop it! You—you suffragette—
[MARY *regards him curiously.*]

MARY

I beg your pardon. I forgot how close you were.
[ARCHIE *strokes the horse.* MARY's *irony melts into
genuine pity.*] Poor you—poor Inches everywhere.
Father and I—we never thought of what it will
mean to *you.*

ARCHIE

What what will mean? [*The horse nuzzles
against his shoulders.*] There, old fellow—it's all
right. There—there—

MARY

Do you really adore them so?

ARCHIE

They're my life, Mary. [*He smiles uncertainly.*] I *might* manage to make friends with engines, if *you* would with *them.*

MARY

I don't say they're not all right in their place, you know—to make pets of, or ride on for pleasure, if you can *call* it pleasure. But they've certainly no business in the city.

ARCHIE

The city's business depends on them.

MARY

The city's for men. Father says men shouldn't depend on anything they can't make for themselves. What if all the horses in the world should get hives, or heaves, or whatever it *is* they get, and die to-morrow? Where'd we be then? We can't make horses. "Beasts of burden," your grandmother. They're the masters now. And they know it. Not much longer, though.

ARCHIE

They're terribly nice, really they are. You don't know them— [*He reaches into his pocket and brings forth a cube of sugar and hands it to her.*] Here— Please— Don't be narrow. Try it—

MARY

Sugar.

ARCHIE

Give him one.
[MARY *looks from the sugar to the horse.*]

MARY

How do you do it?

ARCHIE

—In the flat of your hand—like this— [*He feeds a piece to the horse.*] Bend your fingers back.
[MARY *thrusts the sugar under the horse's nose.*]

MARY

Here, you—sweets to the— [*The horse turns his face to her.*] Heavens! What an outlook! [*The horse stiffens.*] Niiiice Horsie— [*The horse ceases his purring.*] Here, stupid— [*The horse rolls his eyes.*] It isn't poisoned, you know. I hadn't time to poison it. [*Impatiently, she thrusts the sugar against his muzzle.*] Oh, *take* it, you ass!
[*The horse throws his head up.*]

ARCHIE

Don't call him an ass! They don't like that.
[*And indeed the horse looks very angry.* MARY *looks from him to* ARCHIE, *scornfully.*]

MARY

No—? Well he's lucky to get off that easily.
My *real* opinion is that he's neither horse nor ass:
he's a combination. In fact, he's—*ouch!* [*For the
horse has taken advantage of this unguarded moment
to seize the sugar in his mouth, and with it,* MARY's
hand.] Ouch! Ouch! *Ouch!* [*She beats the
beast's head with her free hand. The orchestra begins to play another tune.*] Archie! Archie!

ARCHIE

[*Somewhat alarmed.*]
It's—it's just horse-play.

MARY

[*Shrieking.*]
You *chump,* you!

ARCHIE

P-please don't, Joseph. P-please don't play so
roughly!

MARY

Oh! His teeth! Let go! Let *go!*
   [ARCHIE *seizes the horse's jaws and tries to
   coax them open.*]

ARCHIE

Open! You don't know your strength, Josie.
[*Still the beast holds.*] *Open,* do you hear me?

MARY

Ohhh! What *good* are you?

[*At this,* ARCHIE *throws all reverence to the winds, seizes the animal's ear, pulls his head down and fetches him a brutal kick in the stomach. The horse doubles up, stamps, relinquishes his hold upon* MARY'S *hand and lunges at* ARCHIE, *receiving a blow upon the nose, which finally stills him. He stands panting, rolling his bloodshot eyes wildly.* ARCHIE *takes* MARY *in his arms.*]

ARCHIE

Darling! Darling—

MARY

[*Faintly, against his shoulder.*]
It's—it's all right. Didn't hurt much.

ARCHIE

Mary—I love you so. You're my life, Mary. Your poor hand—let me see—

[*He takes the wrong hand and kisses it.*]

MARY

Here— [*She gives him the right one, he kisses it.*] His teeth are all loose. I could feel them giving. It was horrible.

[ARCHIE *binds her hand with his pocket-handkerchief.*]

ARCHIE

Of course I don't want to make excuses for him. He acted unpardonably. But—but— [*Suddenly he stops, in blank horror.*] Mary!

MARY

What?

ARCHIE

[*Slowly, awfully.*]
I've—beaten—a horse—

MARY

Well, I should hope you had. [*Overcome with remorse,* ARCHIE *feeds a handful of sugar to* JOSEPH, *who devours it eagerly and belches his satisfaction.* MARY *moves Right.*] I'm going to walk home.

ARCHIE

You can't walk with that hand.

MARY

I've got feet, thanks.
[*From off Left comes the sound of a husky bass voice singing "White Wings, They Never Grow Weary."* ARCHIE *urges* MARY *into the cab.*]

ARCHIE

Get in, dear. Here's the cabby.

MARY

Ride behind *that* monster *now?*

ARCHIE

He's sorry. He'll behave. Won't you, Joseph? [*The horse turns his head from them haughtily, nose in the air. The singing draws nearer; "They carry me cheerily over the sea. Night comes, I long for my dearie—"*] Oh, *please,* dear. You must— [*She shakes her head.*] Not afraid, are you? [*She looks at him scornfully, and steps into the cab.*] There. There, *that's* right. Oh, this'll be *peachy!* [*He mounts the steps and bends over her.*] Kiss me, Mary. [*She looks at him, startled, then rises, to leave the cab.*] I said *kiss* me. [*Suddenly she throws her arms about his neck and kisses him. He laughs joyfully.*] There! You *had* to. You wanted to! You'll keep on wanting to—then you'll marry me!

MARY

No—*no*

ARCHIE

Yes—*yes.* I can't ever lose you, now. You may think I can, but I can't. Remember what I said: "They'll never find a better reason!" Oh, Mary— *say* you'll marry me!

MARY

How can I? I don't love you.

ARCHIE

Then—tell me the kind of fellow you think you
might love.
    [*She regards him thoughtfully.*]

MARY

To-morrow—where'll you be about six?

ARCHIE

We're going to take in a new member to-morrow.
After work we'll meet up there on the Parkway for
the ceremony.

MARY

Look for me at six.

ARCHIE

Yes, yes! But tell me what I asked you: the kind
of fellow—

MARY

—Maybe somebody who would drop everything
and—follow my father. I think I might grow very
fond of *him*.

ARCHIE

Where's your father going?

MARY

I told you! To put the cart before the horse.
[*Impulsively.*] Oh, *Archie,* what a chance! What
a chance for any one!

ARCHIE

[*Bewildered.*]
But—

MARY

To-morrow.

[HERBERT, *the cabby, enters along the Parkway,
from Left, in a long coat and a brilliant
papier-mâché topper. Extremely rosy of
complexion and teetering slightly, he continues to roar his song:* "*I sppppreead out my
White Wings, and—*"]

ARCHIE

Herbert, is that you?

[HERBERT *stops dead in his tracks and
focuses.*]

HERBERT

Well, if 'tisn't the Chief!

[*The horse begins to wag its tail joyfully.*]

ARCHIE

[*Severely.*]

Are you the worse for liquor?

[HERBERT *descends the steps into the Boulevard.*]

HERBERT

The worse? Hunnerpercen the better, if you ask me. [*He does a brief clog-step, then whips off his topper.*] Seen my new hat? [*He shows it, proudly.*] —Made of chewed-up paper, varnished. New 'nvention. Sheds the wet. [*With great deliberation he spits upon the hat, wipes it with his sleeve and shows it again.*] See? Couldn't do that with a *silk* hat.

MARY

Let's *start!*

HERBERT

Presently, Miss. [*To* ARCHIE.] I said to your grandpa this morning: "Major," I said—

ARCHIE

We're in a hurry!

HERBERT

This modern generation! Where will you stop?

MARY

When will we *start?*

HERBERT

Presently, Miss, presently—with the help of God.
[*He unfastens the horse's weight, places it
upon the floor below his seat and disdaining
ARCHIE's help, with difficulty mounts the box
and takes the reins. ARCHIE seats himself
beside MARY. The horse cranes his neck
wildly toward them.*]

HERBERT

Cllck—cllck— Giddap! [*The horse does not
move. HERBERT flaps the reins against his back.*]
Giddap, I say!
[*The horse plants his feet, snorting.*]

MARY

Ninny! What's your whip for?

HERBERT

Hush, lady. Don't mention whips. That's Mr.
Inch with you.

ARCHIE

[*Coldly.*]
Well?

[*Whispering.*]

'S a ver' spirited animal, sir. Got pure stallion blood in 'im. [*Coaxingly.*] C'mon now, Josie-boy. Don't make Herbert speak to you again. Cllck! [*The horse stamps, again craning his neck in* MARY'S *direction.* HERBERT *whispers, this time to* JOSEPH.] —This is really embarrassing. What will our fares think of you? Giddap, Josie! [*The horse plants his feet more firmly.* HERBERT *turns to* ARCHIE.] —He acted like this once before, when I had a murderer inside 'n didn't know it. *He* knew, though.

MARY

—And he knows now.

[*She rises but* ARCHIE *forces her into the seat again.*]

ARCHIE

Please— [*He swings himself over the dashboard onto the box.*] Give me the reins. [*He takes the reins from* HERBERT *and pulls them taut.*] Cllck, cllck!

[*No result.* ARCHIE, *in growing anger, saws the bit back and forth.*]

ARCHIE

Now gittap! *Gittap,* I say! [*The horse neighs*

cynically. ARCHIE *rises furiously, seizing the whip.*]
Will you *move!*

> [*He gives the beast one savage lash across the
> back and he begins to move slowly Left, trem-
> bling and snorting.*]

HERBERT

[*Shocked.*]
Why, *Mr.* Inch!—after all he's done for you—

ARCHIE

Shut your trap, or I'll kick you out. [*Between
his teeth, to* MARY.] Poplar Street, did you say?

MARY

A hundred and one.

> [ARCHIE *flaps the reins and the horse begins
> to move faster.* MARY *sits forward on the
> seat, straight as a ramrod.* HERBERT *lifts
> his head and bawls his song, as they drive
> off.*]

HERBERT

"Whiiiite Wings, they nevvur grow weeeary,
They carry me cheerilee ovvur theee sea—
Night comes, I long for my dearieeeeee,
I spprreead out my whiiiite wingssss
An' fly-ee 'ome t' theeeee."

CURTAIN

WHITE WINGS : ACT TWO

ACT II

Scene One

The Parkway, just before six o'clock the following evening. The scene is the reverse of the scene of Act I. In the background are the buildings of a placid, rather attractive little city. In the sky, a pattern of clouds.

The Parkway is a continuous asphalt pavement from Left to Right, with a two-foot stone wall at back. At Left, against this wall, is the rear of the second-story of "The Elite." Also at Left, is a short flight of stone steps, leading down to the Boulevard.

The Parkway is empty, although the head and shoulders of Herbert *are visible above the Parkway wall, as he dozes upon his box in the Boulevard.*

After a moment the sound of wheels is heard approaching from off Right, and Mr. Inch *comes in, pushing his little red cart ahead of him, biting his lip and staring into space. He wears a white*

*duck uniform and a white helmet. Up and down
the left sleeve of his jacket runs an entire column
of service stripes. The cart is marked in white
with a large D.S.C. and his number "2." It con-
tains broom, brush and shovel.* MR. INCH *runs
the cart absently into the curb, leans back against
it, takes off his helmet and disconsolately mops his
brow.*

MR. INCH

Oh, dear—

[*He stands there staring at the pavement, shak-
ing his head sadly. The sound of rapid feet
is heard from off Left, and* MARY *comes
running in, hatless, and carrying a can of
oil. She passes* MR. INCH, *then stops, turns
and faces him. For a moment they gaze at
each other silently.* MARY *smiles.* MR. INCH
returns her smile uncertainly.]

MARY

Hello.

MR. INCH

Hello.

MARY

You're Mr. Inch, aren't you?

MR. INCH

Yes.

MARY

That's nice.
  [MR. INCH *points to the oil-can.*]

MR. INCH

What you got there?

MARY

Here?

MR. INCH

Yes.

MARY

Oil.

MR. INCH

What for?

MARY

Oh—oiling things.

MR. INCH

That's nice.
  [*They gaze at each other for another moment,
    smiling. Then:*]

MARY

[*Sing-song.*]

Well, good-bye—

[MR. INCH *makes a stiff little gesture.* MARY
*turns and runs off Right. Gradually the
smile leaves* MR. INCH's *face. He seats himself upon the curbstone, takes from a bag at-
tached to his cart a cake of sapolio, a can of
water, a small brush and a cloth, and begins
listlessly to polish his shovel. After a moment he stops, and sits staring in front of
him again, a picture of misery.* ARCHIE
*comes pushing his cart in hastily from Right.
He is dressed as his father, but with an insignia upon his helmet, and only two service
stripes upon his sleeve.*]

ARCHIE

Hello, sir! You're ahead of time. I suppose
you've heard it's practically settled about Clyde.

MR. INCH

We're really going to take Clyde Sims on the
Force?

ARCHIE

This afternoon—provided, of course, there's no
hitch in the final proceedings. I don't look for any.
He wrote an excellent paper and has qualified per-

fectly both in straightaway sweeping, and going around lamp-posts.

MR. INCH

Oh, dear, oh, dear.

ARCHIE

What's the matter, sir? You aren't worried about *him?*

MR. INCH

Yes, I am!—Aw, Archie—we'd oughtn't to take on a new man, really we'd oughtn't. And Clyde's too young—he doesn't know his own mind yet—a boy just out of college.

ARCHIE

But his name has been up for years!

MR. INCH

He'd ought to have stuck to the Law, like his father and grandfather.

ARCHIE

The professions are hardly to be compared, Papa.

MR. INCH

He'll never make a White Wing—never in this world.

ARCHIE

On the contrary, he has a genuine talent for it.

MR. INCH

Well, I hope he fails in his test, that's what I hope!

ARCHIE

[*Reprovingly.*]
Why, Father—

MR. INCH

I do!—Oh, I know the glamor our life has for outsiders—but I'm talking from the inside—the way way in inside. [*A brief pause.*] I can't face him. I wish I was some place miles away from here.—I wish I was in Madeira, there's where I wish I was.

[*Archie frowns, puzzled.*]

ARCHIE

Madeira?

MR. INCH

I was reading my Baedeker last night in bed. Baedeker, bed— [*He smiles, foolishly.*] Beddie, —bye, Baedeker—

ARCHIE

Don't be silly, Papa— Has any one been along here looking for me?

MR. INCH

No— One thing about Madeira struck me particularly.

ARCHIE

What?

MR. INCH

There—there aren't any horses there. Archie, I think I'd rather work in Madeira.

ARCHIE

It must be a primitive place. They use oxen, don't they?

MR. INCH

Well, it would be a little change.

ARCHIE

[*Good-humoredly.*]

Change, change! You're forever talking about change.

MR. INCH

Horses, horses—I'm forever following horses— twenty years. You get sort of sick of 'em after twenty years— And all day to-day they've been acting so queerly. It's enough to drive a man crazy.

ARCHIE

You're just tired and nervous. Come, sir—
brace up!

MR. INCH

It's them that are nervous about something.
Twice I was nearly stepped on, and three of 'em bit
at me.

ARCHIE

Maybe there's a thunderstorm coming. They get
them hours before we do.

MR. INCH

There's *something* in the air. *That's* sure— And
I think it's more than a thunderstorm. [*A brief
pause.*] I knew the boy's father. Cornelius Sims
was a fine man. I can't see Clyde do it—I can't! I
can't!

ARCHIE

Shh! The cabby will hear you.

MR. INCH

I don't care!— Anyway, he's asleep.

ARCHIE

I don't pretend to understand your attitude, but
if you don't like your vocation, why not leave it?

MR. INCH

Your mother,—Archie, since she married me, that woman's been more of a White Wing than the White Wings.— And your grandfather—you know how the Major feels— Nope—I can't do it.

ARCHIE

At least you *can* stop criticizing the Service in public. Coming from you—an Inch—think of the effect on the man in the street.

MR. INCH

Listen, Son; when you were a little chap of seven I heard you say to your mother and the Major that sooner than be a White Wing, you'd—

ARCHIE

I am quite content with *my* lot, thank you.

MR. INCH

I don't know what became of that little boy. *He* wasn't content with anything. I had high hopes for that little boy. Life's funny—

ARCHIE

Life's *great!*

MR. INCH

You mean you think it's going to be.

ARCHIE

I *know* it will be.

MR. INCH

The picture man says "See the pretty birdie!—Hear him peep!"— But there isn't ever any pretty birdie—it's a lie, to keep you quiet— You look, though—and you listen—

ARCHIE

Well—?

MR. INCH

—What you see, is a black cloth and a round eye. What you hear, is a click, and a sliding sound.

ARCHIE

It won't be that way for me, nor for Clyde, either.

MR. INCH

Oh, I hope not! [*He sighs*]—I thought I'd find pretty birdies all through my life—[*He turns away*]—I've found sparrows.

ARCHIE

[*Shocked.*]
Father!

MR. INCH

—But I look! I keep looking—

ARCHIE

Yes, and you'll find them yet.

[MR. INCH *shakes his head*.]

MR. INCH

—They're never in the same place twice. I'm always in the same place.

ARCHIE

[*Cheerfully*.]

The world's moving, sir. You move with it.

MR. INCH

No, Son—nor do you. We run backwards, we Inches. It slides under our feet. We're always just where we started. [*He grasps* ARCHIE'S *arm*.] Oh, if ever you get a chance to turn round, take it, Son! Don't wait till your old legs won't run but one way. [*He shakes the arm*]— Pretty birdies, ahead, Archie! Behind—sparrows, sparrows—

[ARCHIE *laughs nervously*.]

ARCHIE

Really, Papa, you're—

[MR. INCH *suddenly becomes furious*.]

MR. INCH

Don't you "really" me! [*He softens again as suddenly*.] Aw, Archie—you're just a child.— So is Clyde. Why don't you see things as they are, like children do? Why don't you call 'em their right names? [*He pronounces deliberately.*] "Street-cleaners."

ARCHIE

White Wings!
[MR. INCH *stamps his foot.*]

MR. INCH

Street-cleaners! Street-cleaners!
[*From off Right comes the sound of approaching voices and cart-wheels. ARCHIE takes his father's arm.*]

ARCHIE

Come along with me. The men mustn't see you like this.

MR. INCH

I don't care.—Street-cleaners!

ARCHIE

Come now—come—
[*He hurries him off Left, stopping for a moment to place the cart beside his own. From Left, in single file, enters the THREE WHITE WINGS. They are dressed as ARCHIE and his father, but with varying numbers of service*]

*stripes, two of them with no insignia upon
their helmets, and the third with a black
derby hat in place of a helmet, and no number-
badge. The little red carts each contain a
broom, brush and shovel, are marked with the
white "D.S.C.," and numbered "51," "114"
and "9." PAUL PILLSBURY comes first,
whistling a popular song of the period. He
is 35, RALPH OTIS is 30, and CLYDE SIMS,
3rd, is 22. PAUL bumps his cart into place
beside ARCHIE's and MR. INCH's. RALPH and
CLYDE do the same. CLYDE's cart and im-
plements have seen very little use.*]

PAUL

Ooomph!

RALPH

What a day.

CLYDE

Gracious, it's hot.

PAUL

Do you suppose it's the heat that's started them
off?

RALPH

—The horses?— Can't tell, when they get spells

like this.   One of 'em goes funny for some reason
of his own, and the rest of 'em catch it.

> [PAUL *and* RALPH *take sapolio, cloths and*
> *brushes from the bags attached to their carts,*
> *seat themselves and begin industriously*
> *polishing their shovels.* CLYDE *leans over the*
> *wall, watching the crowds pass in the street*
> *below.*]

PAUL

There was a ring around the moon last night.

RALPH

I knew a man once, and a meteor fell in his back-
yard.   Three weeks later his grandmother died in
Duluth.

> [HERBERT *suddenly starts up from his box and*
> *calls to an unseen individual.*]

HERBERT

Cab?   Cab, sir?   [*A brief pause.   Hope dies in*
his face.   He reseats himself.]   All right.   Walk.

> [*Another pause.*   CLYDE *leans further out over*
> *the wall, raises his derby, waves his hand, then*
> *turns to* PAUL *and* RALPH.]

CLYDE

—Mrs. Mendlessohn—   My, she's got fat.

PAUL

Rubberneck.

RALPH

Stretch it.

PAUL

Throw it up and catch it.
[CLYDE *looks a little hurt.*]

RALPH

You'd better quit mashing and fix your cart. The Major's due in five minutes.

PAUL

You're not *on* the Force yet, you know.

CLYDE

I shall be this afternoon.

RALPH

Maybe.

CLYDE

I guess I got a B-plus on my paper.

PAUL

The written test is pie, compared to the oral.

RALPH

I'll never forget the day *I* came up against the Major.   I thought it was back to the Bank for me.

PAUL

Better not be over-confident, Sims—or you may have to find another way to land that rich wife you're after.

CLYDE

I don't know what you mean.

RALPH

Oh, we're on to you!— You're in this job for the runaways you can stop, and nothing else.

CLYDE

That's a lie!
   [RALPH *and* PAUL *laugh.*]

RALPH

—Anyway, take my advice and don't let the Chief see the way you use your instruments.

PAUL

—Shoveling against the broom—lah-dee-dah, lah-dee-dah—

CLYDE

But it's the proper way! I know it is.

PAUL

You amateurs have grand theories.

RALPH

Listen, Candidates: you may shovel against the broom in the laboratory, but in the street you brush into the shovel.

CLYDE

You're just trying to confuse me! [RALPH *shrugs.* CLYDE *becomes anxious.*] Look here: isn't this right? Broom—shovel— [*He makes a gesture of sweeping and emptying*]—dump.

[RALPH *goes through his motions.*]

RALPH

—Shovel—*broom*—dump. [*And* PAUL *through his, by way of confirmation.* CLYDE *looks off Left, then sounds a low, intense warning.*]

CLYDE

Cheese it! Cheese it, the Chief!

[PAUL *and* RALPH *throw startled glances off Left, then all quickly seat themselves upon the curbstone and begin polishing their shovels furiously.*]

HERBERT

Cab? Cab, sir? Here you are, sir—*open* cab!

[*A tense moment, then* HERBERT *smiles, leans forward, takes the blanket from his horse's back, folds it up, seizes the reins and whip and moves off Left, to the accompaniment of rumbling wheels.* ARCHIE *comes in Left, followed by* MR. INCH. ARCHIE *watches the* WHITE WINGS *silently for a moment. Then:*]

ARCHIE

Sims—

[CLYDE *looks up, inquiringly.*]

—Rub with the grain. You'll find it easier.

CLYDE

Yes, sir.

ARCHIE

[*Going to him.*]

You have all my best wishes, Sims.

[CLYDE *takes his hand, gratefully.*]

CLYDE

Th-thank you, sir.

[MR. INCH, *with broom and shovel, removes odds and ends from the pavement.* ARCHIE *looks out over the wall, glances at his watch, then turns to* RALPH.]

ARCHIE

Major Inch has already left Headquarters.   We
may expect him at any moment.   Oh, Ralph—

RALPH

Yes, Chief?

ARCHIE

Has any one inquired for me?

RALPH

I don't think so.
    [*He looks to* PAUL.]

PAUL

—No.   No one's been by at all.
    [KIT CANARI *enters from Right, on a bicycle.*
    He is a little older than ARCHIE, *well-dressed,*
    attractively homely, and with an air of being
    much amused with life.]
Well—get on to the scorcher!

KIT

Hello, Archie.

ARCHIE

Hello, Kit.

KIT

How's the Spick-and-Span Brigade?
[*He dismounts, rests his bicycle against the wall, removes his trousers-guards and puts them in his pocket.*]

ARCHIE

—Men, this is my friend, Mr. Christopher Canari.

KIT

Hello, boys.

PAUL

How do you do.

RALPH

[*Simultaneously.*]
Glad to meet you.

CLYDE

[*Simultaneously.*]
Charmed, I'm sure.
[KIT *flips a cigarette butt to the pavement.* MR. INCH *sweeps it up, protesting:*]

MR. INCH

Hey! Hey!

KIT

[*To* ARCHIE.]

I just saw that little What's-her-name you took
home last night.

[MR. INCH *prods the bicycle with his shovel.*]

ARCHIE

[*Very casually.*]

Oh— Nice child. Where was she?

KIT

—Hurrying down Poplar Street with a can of
oil— Shouted something over her shoulder about
being up here at six, to see history made.—
Through with work, are you?

[*He glances into the carts.* ARCHIE *looks over
the wall.*]

ARCHIE

—Afraid not— I never saw so many gigs out.
It looks like a little overtime to-night!— Lord!—
Is that Mother? [*He turns anxiously to* CLYDE.]
Sims, I'll never forgive myself: when a final candi-
date receives his helmet, it is customary to—

CLYDE

—The flowers for Mrs. Inch. I know, sir. I
have them.

[ARCHIE *sighs in relief.*]

ARCHIE

Thank heaven! Up, men—up!

[*Up the stairs from the Boulevard, comes* Mrs.
Fanny Inch, *a plain and forceful woman of
about forty. She is dressed in her finest and
carries a parasol and a large net bag containing a new* White Wing's *helmet, wrapped
in tissue-paper. The* White Wings *rise, uncover, and stand stiffly at attention.* Mrs.
Inch *goes to* Archie *and kisses him on both
cheeks.*]

MRS. INCH

Dear boy—

ARCHIE

This is Kit Canari, Mother.

MRS. INCH

One of the Boston Canaris?

KIT

I'm afraid not.

MRS. INCH

Never mind. Family isn't everything. [*She
turns to the* White Wings, *smiling her most social
smile and working her eyebrows slightly.*] Won't
you sit down? [*All sit and continue their polishing*

except CLYDE. MRS. INCH *turns to him.*]. Well,
Clyde—how does it feel?

CLYDE

[*Overcome.*]
Mrs. Inch— I—

MRS. INCH

[*Tenderly.*]
I know. I know. Don't try to say it. What a
day this is for all of us. How happy your dear
father and mother would be. But they know—you
may be sure they know, Clyde.— Now we must see
that everything about you is just letter-perfect.
[*She fusses over him.*] The Major is most
punctilious about details. I often say, no woman
was ever more finicky. If he— [CLYDE *is staring
anxiously off Left. Suddenly he starts and gasps.*]

CLYDE
—The Major! He's here!— And I've forgotten
everything!

MRS. INCH
It will come back. Be calm—just be calm.

ARCHIE
Fall in!

[*The* WHITE WINGS *form themselves into a
line facing front, each beside his cart, each
with his broom upon his shoulder.* MR. INCH
*is at the Left end of the line, with his broom
against the wrong shoulder.* ARCHIE *is at
the Right end, a step in advance of the
others. From Left, enters* MAJOR PHILIP
INCH *in a resplendent white uniform, with
many service chevrons, a Phi Beta Kappa
Key, and a Carnegie Medal or so. He is
about seventy, distinguished in appearance,
and very much impressed with himself. He
carries a thin copy-book with blue covers,
of the sort used in college examinations. The
line of* WHITE WINGS *stiffens.* ARCHIE *gives
the command.*]

'Ten—shun! [*The line becomes even more rigid.
A salute is given, and returned by the* MAJOR.
ARCHIE *speaks in a stilted voice, eyes straight
ahead.*] Good afternoon, Grandfather.

MAJOR INCH

Afternoon. [*He bows to* MRS. INCH, *who returns
his bow.*] —Fanny. [*She takes the new helmet
from her bag and unwraps it. The* MAJOR *goes to*
MR. INCH *and murmurs softly:*] Will you never
learn? [*He changes the broom to the right shoulder,
pokes* MR. INCH's *stomach in, grunts and centers his
attention upon* CLYDE.] Is this the new man?

ARCHIE

Yes, sir. Clyde Sims, Third, sir.

MAJOR INCH

[*To* CLYDE.]
Do you know who I am?

CLYDE

Yes, sir. Major Philip Inch, sir. I have heard
of you in connection with the march upon Antietam.

MAJOR INCH

[*Softening.*]
It was nothing. [*To* ARCHIE.] Did you tell
him about my wounds?

ARCHIE

No, sir.
[MAJOR INCH *removes his helmet, advances to*
CLYDE, *bows his head and parts the hair
upon his scalp.*]

CLYDE

[*Sympathetically.*]
Tsch—tsch—tsch—
[MAJOR INCH *steps back and replaces the hel-
met upon his head.*]

MAJOR INCH

It was nothing. [*He opens the blue book and glances over it.*] Hum . . . hum. . . . Your paper is not bad, not at all bad. But as to the derivation of my name, "Philip," you say merely that it is from the Greek. That is hardly adequate. Well?

CLYDE

"Philos" and " 'ippos." . . .

MAJOR INCH

Meaning?

CLYDE

"The lover of a horse."

[MAJOR INCH *looks suspiciously to* ARCHIE.]

MAJOR INCH

You told him.

ARCHIE

No, sir. Really.

[*The blue book is handed to him, and is passed down the line to* MR. INCH, *who drops it into his cart.*]

MAJOR INCH

[*To* MRS. INCH.]

The helmet—

MRS. INCH

[*In a whisper, to* CLYDE.]
The flowers—

> [*She gives* MAJOR INCH *the new helmet.* CLYDE
> *reaches into the depths of his cart, brings
> forth a bouquet of flowers with trailing rib-
> bons and presents it to* MRS. INCH.]

MRS. INCH

Oh, thank you—thank you, Clyde.

> [MAJOR INCH *sets the helmet upon* CLYDE's
> *head.*]

MAJOR INCH

This is merely for size. You are prepared for
the oral test?

CLYDE

I am, sir.

> [MAJOR INCH *advances, opens* CLYDE's *mouth
> and peers into it.*]

MAJOR INCH

Say "Ah." . . .

CLYDE

Ahhhhh.

> [MAJOR INCH *releases him.*]

MAJOR INCH

Hum. [*He bends over, picks up* CLYDE's *foot, gazes at the sole of his shoe, then drops it again.*] Hum. [*A brief pause.*] And cough. [CLYDE *coughs.*] Any pain?

CLYDE

Not a bit, sir.

MAJOR INCH

[*Suddenly.*]
Who is your favorite poet?

CLYDE

Horace.

MAJOR INCH

—Character in history?

CLYDE

Paul Revere.

MAJOR INCH

—Regular Know-it-all, aren't you? Well, answer me this, if you can: If a farmer has a stud-farm which produces two crops of studs per season, how many—

[*He is interrupted by the wild entrance from Left, in the street below, of* HERBERT, *in head-and-shoulders.* JOSEPH *is apparently running away with him. He is hatless, tugging at the reins, and bawling breathlessly:*]

HERBERT

Whoa! Whoa! Damn you! Whoa! *Whoa!* You crazy coot—

ARCHIE

Fall out!

[ARCHIE *and the* WHITE WINGS *fly to the wall.* KIT *follows.* JOSEPH, *crazed with fright, is doing his best to climb over the wall into the Parkway.*]

MRS. INCH

Joseph! Stop that! What are you thinking of?

HERBERT

Git down, you! Hey! Git *down!*

MAJOR INCH

Drop that whip!

[JOSEPH *is finally quieted without further recourse to the whip.*]

PAUL

What happened?

HERBERT

—There on Elm Street—red buckboard—some one's unhitched the horse—it was coasting along by itself.

[PAUL *grunts.*]

KIT

No wonder your plug was scared.

HERBERT

[*In an awestruck voice.*]
—And they was people in it—man and young woman.

MRS. INCH

—No one we know, I hope.

CLYDE

Gracious—weren't they simply panicky?

HERBERT

[*More awesomely still.*]
They was laughing—   [*Then, vindictively.*]
But maybe by this time—   [*With relish.*]   —Maybe that laugh's stilled forever.

ARCHIE

[*Sharply.*]
How could—how could a carriage coast on *Elm* Street? It's flat as your hand.

HERBERT

Then somebody 'gin it one hell of a shove.

KIT

Elm near Poplar?

HERBERT

Just round the corner. [*Suddenly* KIT *snaps his fingers excitedly and runs off Left.*] —An' Josie wasn't the only one it scared, neither. Altogether, I saw six bolt.

CLYDE

Six! That's a *lot*. Some one ought to—

MAJOR INCH

Fall in! [*The White Wings obey. But suddenly something in the Boulevard below catches the* MAJOR'S *eye. He freezes in his tracks, his eyes bulging. Distant shouts are heard off Right. The* MAJOR *gasps:*] Oh, my God!

   [*The shouts and general confusion come nearer. The White Wings stand at attention, all eyes forward.*]

ARCHIE

   [*In measured tones.*]
What—is—it—Grandfather—?
   [*The* MAJOR *does not answer. Instead, he*

[*braces himself against the wall and gazes down into the street. Dogs bark, women scream, the pandemonium increases. HER-BERT is having a difficult time holding his horse, for at least three runaways are taking place.*]

MAJOR INCH

My God. My God.

[*MR. INCH passes a nervous hand across his forehead. He is breathing hard. Suddenly, through the uproar, a steady "chug-chug" makes itself heard. Then:*]

ARCHIE

[*Sharply.*]

Fall out!

[*In an instant the line breaks and the White Wings are staring over the wall, MR. INCH endeavoring to push through them into a place.*]

MR. INCH

What is it? What is it?

RALPH

Heavens alive!

[*PAUL whistles his astonishment.*]

MRS. INCH

[*Simultaneously.*]

Mercy! Mercy on us!

MR. INCH

I want to see! I want to see! [ARCHIE *turns and he and* RALPH *lift him up on their shoulders.*] Why—why, it's coasting *up hill!*

MAJOR INCH

Don't be ridiculous.

MR. INCH

But look, Papa, look!

MRS. INCH

I've seen that man before.

MR. INCH

Why, it's Charlie Todd! [*He pulls his hat off and waves it excitedly.*] Hi, there! Hello, Charlie!
    [*The* MAJOR *reaches up and drags him to the ground.* ARCHIE *stands like a statue, staring fixedly into the street.* MR. INCH *endeavors again to get through the line to the wall, but without success.*]

MRS. INCH

He's got a young girl with him.

[*All eyes are now turned toward the Right.*]

MAJOR INCH

It's—it's turning up here!

[ARCHIE *wheels about suddenly.*]

ARCHIE

Men—fall in!

CLYDE

There's a runaway nobody's paying any attention to!

[*He is about to vault the wall.*]

ARCHIE

Sims!— Did you hear me? [CLYDE *reluctantly falls in.* MR. INCH *springs into his place at the wall.*] Inch!

MAJOR INCH

I'm in command. You forget yourself.

ARCHIE

Fall in, I say! [*The* MAJOR *falls in.* ARCHIE *turns to* MR. INCH.] Inch! [MR. INCH *falls in. The line is now complete.*] Left wheel! [*The line*

wheels and forms a cordon across the road.]   Still
pond! [*The line halts.*]   No more moving!
   [*There is an anxious pause.*]

MR. INCH

I—I'm not happy here.

CLYDE

We'll die like rats.

ARCHIE

Shut up!

MR. INCH

My heart's going like anything.
   [*The uproar from below diminishes, but the
   steady "chug-chug" increases ominously in
   volume from the Right.*]

ARCHIE

Steady, men.   Keep your line!   Stand your
ground! Don't budge!
   [*The line stands firm. At last, from Right, in
   chugs the first horseless carriage, with* MR.
   CHARLIE TODD, *a cheery individual of about
   forty-six, smiling his elation at the steering-
   bar. Beside him sits* MARY, *her head proudly
   in the air.* MAJOR INCH *pipes out:*]

MAJOR INCH

Stop!

MR. TODD

Oh, I can, easily. All you do is this— [*He reaches for a lever, and with a grinding of brakes the buggy halts. Mrs.* INCH *screams in alarm, and the line of White Wings breaks.* MR. TODD *smiles indulgently upon* MRS. INCH.] —Keep your shirt on, Mrs. Inch. I warned you of this years ago.

MRS. INCH

Then it *is* Charlie Todd—Todd, the furnace-man! [MR. TODD *rises from his seat and bows.*]

MR. TODD

Clinkers painlessly removed. [*He claps his hands together and begins a spiel in the manner of a circus-barker.*] *Now* then, Ladies and Gents, gather right around. Step right up, Ladies and Gents, Gents and Ladies—view the horseless buggy—the automatic buckboard—see the wunnerful, maaahhh-veelous, in-cred-i-ble, mee-rack-elous manner 'n' wich this modern little gig skips along without a hoss. Hear her snort an' snap an' stutter! Watch her skip an' scat an' scutter! Some one asks what makes her go? Well, 'neath the seat, upon a treadmill walk ten thousand young red ants! In my hand I hold a pepper-pot of Potter's Best Red Pepper!

The more pepper I give 'em, the faster they go!
The more—

Charlie Todd, you aren't being open with us.

Why, Mrs. Inch, I'd no more try to deceive a lady
like you, than I'd slit my own mother's throat. Why,
I'd sooner—
[*He touches something and the buggy jumps
forward.*]

That's the ticket!

[*Simultaneously.*]
Heavens save us, Jefferson Davis!
[*She retreats.*]

Pardon me, ma'am, but your placket's open.
[*She clutches at it.*]

[*Admiringly.*]
Is it your own invention, Charlie?

MR. TODD

A fellow in Rochester—he got his patent in first.

MARY

Wouldn't that jar you?

MR. TODD

Yes—but mine *runs*. So patents be damned!

MARY

Look and wonder, People, 'cause we can't stay long.

MR. TODD

Nope—can't stay long. Restless little buggy, this—

MARY

—Won't stand still.

MR. TODD

Won't stand still.

MAJOR INCH

"Horseless"? Horseless hell, sir! *We* know the horse is somewhere!

MR. TODD

—Just the point, Major—

Scene from Act II

MARY

—From now on, the horse is nowhere!
  [*She is looking at* ARCHIE, *who stands like a
    graven image.*]

KIT

  [*To* ARCHIE.]
Right!— Horse is nowhere from now on.

MARY

—And a good thing, too.

MR. INCH

You don't like horses?

MARY

I hate horses!
  [*An awful pause. Then:*]

MAJOR INCH

  [*Heavily.*]
God forgive you, child.

PAUL

It's a crazy-looking little dingus.

CLYDE

Horrid color.

RALPH

Umph! Smells to heaven!

MRS. INCH

I noticed that, too.

MR. TODD

You didn't!

MRS. INCH

I've got a nose. It's an affront.

MR. TODD

—Just the place for it. [*She turns from him, insulted.*] Oh, Mrs. Inch— [*She glances over her shoulder.*] —Placket. [*She arranges it once more.*] —Still living in the same place, Mr. Inch?

MR. INCH

Same old place, Charlie.

[PAUL, RALPH *and* CLYDE *are examining the vehicle curiously.*]

MR. TODD

—I can see it now—the iron deer in the front yard—that back parlor, where Mrs. Inch used to call down the register: "Oh, Mr. Todd! Mr. Toh-od! Will you send up a little more heat?"— And those ancestors on the walls, all in uniform.

The biggest of the lot was the Major himself—and on horseback, at that—where'd you get that horse, Major?

MAJOR INCH

I rented it.

MR. TODD

[*To* MARY.]
—The portrait is entitled "Philip E. Inch, on his Favorite Mount, 'Esquire.' "

MAJOR INCH

[*Stiffly.*]
I was founding a family. I knew what was proper.

MR. TODD

[*To* MARY.]
—A speaking likeness—he has a *beautiful* seat.

MAJOR INCH

I have heard it said that one would think I was part of the horse.

[MARY *laughs suddenly.*]

MR. TODD

Hush, my dear—this is no time for fooling. [*He descends from his perch to the pavement.*] —Nice job, eh, Mr. Inch?

MR. INCH

D—Does it go fast?

MARY

Well, I *started* with a hat on.
[*She gets out of the auto-buggy and faces*
ARCHIE, *triumphantly.*]

MR. TODD

—Speed?   [*Gloating.*]   We passed Willie Titt-
man's mare!

MARY

Well, what do you think of it, Archie?

ARCHIE

I—It's—
[*He cannot go on.*]

MR. INCH

—But what does make it go?

MR. TODD

—Not oats.   *That's* sure.   No—nor red pepper.
Gasoline, that's what—gasoline and erl—

MARY

Oil.

MR. TODD

Erl.

MARY

Oil.

MR. TODD

Erl.

KIT

[*Echoing:*]
—Gasoline and erl.
[*There is an awful silence, as the import of this
    sinks in. Then the* MAJOR *demands
    hoarsely:*]

MAJOR INCH

Men—if this thing succeeds, do you know what
it means for us? [*The White Wings' faces become
very grave. He concludes.*] —It means extinction.
[MR. INCH *is endeavoring to keep his feet from
    dancing.*]

ARCHIE

But it won't succeed!

MARY

[*Flaring up.*]
Who says it won't?

ARCHIE

—An impersonal machine—it can never in this world supplant a noble creature like the horse.

MR. TODD

Can't, eh?

MARY

Watch it!

MR. TODD

Good-bye, you fine sorrels! Good-bye, you sleek roan mares! You hacks, you plugs, you pacers!

MARY

Charlie Todd's done for you!

MR. TODD

God be with you in the boneyard!

MRS. INCH

Take your blasphemies out of our sight!

MR. TODD

Why, Mrs. Inch!— You wouldn't let a mere economic revolution come between *us?* [*She turns away. He continues gleefully.*] Oh, we'll build 'em little and we'll build 'em big! The streets'll be full of 'em! We'll build palaces on wheels, and we'll build cottages! By God, we'll build tin shacks for the men who lug dinner-pails!

KIT

[*To* ARCHIE.]
You know, it's so crazy it must be true.

ARCHIE

But it isn't true. It can't be true.

MR. TODD

Archie, I can't understand you at all. Of course, I do remember that as a kid no bigger than that, you did use to run around the back parlor in a white-duck suit, after a wooden horse named Dobbin your papa pulled on a string—

MR. INCH

Easy there, Charlie.

MR. TODD

—With a big pair of paper wings hitched onto your shoulders. But that was before you'd ever seen the real White Wings at work. You thought they were marvelous beings that soared up and down the Boulevard, over the horses' heads, beating up a breeze that kept the city spick and span.

MR. INCH

—Fanny and the Major.   They let him think it.

MR. TODD

—But that was only until your seventh birthday, when as a great treat, your grandpa took you out to see them actually at it.

MR. INCH

Charlie—

MRS. INCH

As if a child's mistake mattered now.

MR. TODD

—When I saw you streaking back down the street with the Major hot after you, I came upstairs. There was your mother waiting for you with a lovely birthday present—a shiny little cart, and a tiny broom and shovel. Well, you didn't say much when you saw 'em. You couldn't, you were crying so hard. But the Major got the pieces of that shovel straight in the stomach and Dobbin you kicked clear across the room into a bowl of goldfish. You seem to have changed, Archie.

MR. INCH

It's education did it.   Fanny and the Major.
   [ARCHIE *looks at them.*]

MRS. INCH

We gave him the best there was in us. He learned once more to respect tradition and love horses.

MAJOR INCH

We spared no effort to make him every inch an Inch.

MRS. INCH

Yes, and we succeeded!

MR. TODD

Wonderful thing, education. [HERBERT *spits deliberately over the wall into one of the carts.*] Listen, Archie, I'm going to manufacture these buggies on a big scale; eventually I aim to turn out two a month. That'll take capital. To-morrow morning early we leave on a tour to find it. I want some one to go along—some one who looks so far ahead he can't see the horizon. Mary says you're my man. Will you come with us?

ARCHIE

Thank you. Thank you very much. But I can't. [MRS. INCH *and* MAJOR INCH *draw breaths of relief.* MR. INCH *shakes his head, sadly.* MARY *shuts her eyes.*]

KIT

Can't? Well, of all the poor lobsters! *Why* can't you?

ARCHIE

[*After a moment.*]

—Because I don't believe in it.

[MR. TODD *glances at* MARY. *She averts her head.* ARCHIE *looks at his feet.*]

MR. TODD

I'm sorry you don't, Archie. I'm very sorry. I hoped you would.

ARCHIE

It's the horse I believe in.

[KIT *advances eagerly.*]

KIT

Will you take me, sir? I'm Kit Canari. I'd go to hell in that gig.

[MR. TODD *hesitates.*]

RALPH

[*Growling.*]

Bet you would. Damned cigarette-smoker.

MARY

[*Sharply, painfully.*]

Take him!

MR. TODD

[*To* KIT.]

Five-thirty in the morning. Hundred and one Poplar.

MARY

Let him come along now.

KIT

Bye-bye, Archie. You can have my bicycle. [*To* MR. TODD:] All right, sir. Any time you're ready.

> [MR. TODD *cranks. The auto-buggy starts feebly, then stalls dead.*]

MR. TODD

Hum.

PAUL

[*Without a smile.*]

Ha-ha.

> [MR. TODD *scratches his head.*]

MR. TODD

Perhaps the gasoline. [*He peers into the gasoline tank.*] Plenty of gasoline. [*He begins to crank again.*] Oh, yes! The erl—

> [*He crawls under the car.*]

CLYDE

Isn't he agile!

[MR. TODD *reëmerges from beneath the car, his face smudged and unhappy.*]

MR. TODD

Lots of erl.

MRS. INCH

Apparently.

MR. INCH

[*Reflectively.*]
No waste products.

MAJOR INCH

Oh—Herbert—

HERBERT

—A little towin' job? Sure! *I* ain't proud.

[*He takes the reins and prepares to come to the rescue. MR. TODD cranks again, without results. MAJOR INCH, MRS. INCH and the WHITE WINGS look intensely pleased.*]

RALPH

It's simply shot its bolt.

MR. TODD

Probably needs a new mainspring.

PAUL

Drag it off.

HERBERT

Horseless wagon! That's good, that is! [*He laughs.*] —Only you better get a horse.

PAUL

Yea! Get a horse!

RALPH AND CLYDE

Get a horse!
[HERBERT *and his cab move off Right in the Boulevard below.*]

ARCHIE

Here, Mr. Todd—let me.

MARY

[*Sharply.*]
No! No! He shan't touch it!
[KIT *advances.*]

KIT

Give me a try, sir.
[*He spins the crank. There is a faint chug-chug.*]

MR. TODD

That's it! Now we've got it. [*But the chugging dies.*] That—that sounded final.

MARY

Oh, hell.

MAJOR INCH

Oh, Todd—

MR. TODD

[*Impatiently.*]
What? What?

MAJOR INCH

I've called a cab. Just in case.

KIT

Don't be discouraged, sir. As big a thing as this, you know—it's bound to take time.

MR. TODD

Yes—yes, of course.
[MARY *has taken a coil of rope from the front of the auto-buggy. She turns contemptuously to* ARCHIE.]

MARY

Good-bye, you—

ARCHIE

Mary— Oh, this can't make any *real* difference!

MARY

I hope you'll be comfortable, in your casket.
[*She turns away.*] Sympathy from a friend. —Get
in, Father. Canari and I will tie it.

> [MR. TODD *mounts the buggy and takes the
> steering-bar.* MARY *and* KIT *tie one end of
> the rope to the back axle. The cab backs in
> from Left, and is brought to a halt in the
> proper position.*]

HERBERT

[*To the horse.*]
That's right. Now just hold that.

> [KIT *and* MARY *fasten the other end of the
> rope to the cab-axle.*]

MAJOR INCH

Can you take us, as well, Herbert?

HERBERT

Get right in, Major—you'll give Josie confidence.

MAJOR INCH

Fanny—

> [*He hands* MRS. INCH *in and takes his seat be-
> side her.*]

MRS. INCH

I could see at once it wasn't practical.

MAJOR INCH

Supplant the horse, indeed!

HERBERT

Ready there?

KIT

Go ahead.

[*With a great flourish,* HERBERT *cracks his whip, the cab starts, and slowly the entire caravan begins to move off Left,* HERBERT *upon the box, the* MAJOR *and* MRS. INCH *in the cab, the auto-buggy, with* MR. TODD *sitting grimly at the steering-bar, and on foot behind it,* MARY *and* KIT. ARCHIE *watches the departure sadly, the* WHITE WINGS *with delight—*CLYDE *shouts after them.*]

CLYDE

Come again, some day!

PAUL

Only bring your own horse!

RALPH

Yea! Get a horse!

[*Only* KIT *and* MARY *are now left in view.*
KIT *takes* MARY'S *arm comfortingly through
his. She turns and confronts the* WHITE
WINGS.]

MARY

You!— You *sparrows*—
[*A brief silence. Then:*]

CLYDE

[*Gently.*]
Get a horse?
[MARY *and* KIT *follow the auto-buggy off, and
the* WHITE WINGS *follow them, calling in
louder and louder chorus:*]

WHITE WINGS

Get a horse! Get a horse! Get a horse!
[ARCHIE *and* MR. INCH *are left alone in the
street, looking after them.*]

CURTAIN

ACT II

Scene Two

The Parkway about seven o'clock of an autumn evening several years later. The city in the background has undergone several changes and taken on something of the appearance of a manufacturing town, but the pattern of clouds in the sky has not changed. A long window has been cut in the back wall of "The Elite." As it grows darker in the course of the scene, this window is illuminated by a bluish light, from a mercury-lamp within the building, which is now a garage. The Parkway is illuminated by a segment of light cast by an off-stage arc-light, nearby, at Left. Against the Parkway wall stand three little red carts, each with its broom, brush and shovel. HERBERT'S cab stands in its old place in the Boulevard, but HERBERT, now somewhat dilapidated, is seated upon the wall, whip in hand.

At Right, directly in the middle of the Parkway, a square has been roped off around what appears to be the unfinished foundation for a monument of some sort. A lighted red lantern warns of danger here.

114

HERBERT *is telling a story to* JOSEPH, *who listens sympathetically, his head lifted into full view from behind the wall.*

HERBERT

"—An' have you got a ca-ar?" asks Mike. "Shure!" says Pat. "What make is it?" asks Mike. "I ca-al it 'Teddy'," says Pat. "Why 'Teddy'?" asks Mike. [*He leans over the side of the cab, spits into the street, wipes his mouth with the back of his hand, and chuckles.*] "Because," says Pat, "because it's the Roughest Rider ivver was ma-ade!" [*From* JOSEPH *comes a long-drawn gurgling whinny of pleasure, a horse-laugh, in which* HERBERT *joins. Then* JOSEPH *makes an interrogation, to which* HERBERT *responds.*] Yeah-eh—I know *your* parlor-stories! [*A narrative neighing begins, with pauses and inflections.* HERBERT *listens attentively.*] Yea-eh— [*More neighing.* HERBERT *nods.*] Yea-eh— [*More neighing.* HERBERT *interrupts.*] —In a band, you mean—? —Or with a line o' goods? [*An explanatory neigh, then a narrative one.* HERBERT *interrupts again.*] —Springfield, *Massachusetts?* [*A short neigh, then the narrative continues, with many suggestive inflections.*] With a bath? [JOSEPH *replies in the affirmative.*] —And what did *she* say? [JOSEPH *concludes his story.*] Oh, Josie! Josie! [*Both* HERBERT *and* JOSEPH *laugh with great relish.*] Well, you cer-

tainly get the brass-ring, Josie. [*He pushes* Joseph's *head down, controls his mirth and wipes his
eyes.*] My oh me. My oh me. Times has changed,
Josie—changed cruel. [*He becomes a little sad.*]
Yea-eh—we got plenty o' time to sit around crackin'
jokes now. Six fares in two days. Six fares. [*He
sighs.*] My oh me. My oh me. Remember when—?
Oh, well— [*A pause. He begins listlessly to play
with his whip, finally attempting, with a weak gesture, to crack it. It does not crack. He tries again
—and again. It does not crack. He lets the end
drag forlornly over the side, drops his head upon his
breast, and sighs again.*] My oh me. [*A pause,
then:*] What's o'clock?

> [*A hoof is heard to tap seven times upon the
> pavement.*]

HERBERT

—Seven. Yep—there's the lights— [*The arc-
light comes on, off Left.*] We'll wait awhile longer.
Nights like this brings 'em out. [*He takes the butt
of a cigar from his hat and lights it. From Left,
Mr. Inch enters, bearing a block of marble in his
arms. He crosses with it to the foundation and rests
it there, panting. Herbert speaks.*] Could I help
you, sir?

> [Mr. Inch *starts and gasps. Then:*]

MR. INCH

Oh—it's only you.

HERBERT

Could I be of any help, sir?

MR. INCH

Shhh! Not so loud!— Come here— [HERBERT *descends from the wall and goes to him.*] We've got to be careful, Herbert, I'm sure they've got wind of it.

HERBERT

Who? Wind o' what? What's this place roped off for, Mr. Inch? What was you and Mr. Archie doin' here this mornin'?

MR. INCH

Shhh!

HERBERT

There's no one about, sir.

MR. INCH

You can't tell—we think they've been watching. *You're* with us, aren't you, Herbert?

HERBERT

Now as always, sir.

MR. INCH

Then help me set this in place. [*He and* HERBERT *set the block into the corner of the foundation.*] There—! Does it look straight to you?

HERBERT

Straight's a die, sir. But what is it?

MR. INCH

It's the cornerstone.

HERBERT

Cornerstone!— For what, Mr. Inch?

MR. INCH

This— [*He looks about him furtively.*] —The Major Philip E. Inch Memorial White Marble Drinking-Fountain for Horses.

HERBERT

[*In awe.*]

No! So that's it! Ah, what a noble notion! And right here at the very gates of the Park! What a grand situation, sir.

MR. INCH

Will it keep them out, do you think?

HERBERT

The autos? Sure, sir! Sure it will! Better than any City Ordinance ever could!

MR. INCH

The Park is our last stronghold, Herbert—we can't give up the Park without a struggle.

HERBERT

It's the real Inch spirit you have, sir.

MR. INCH

I'm so afraid they'll try to stop it some way. I hope not. This unveiling—it—it means a great deal to us, Herbert, or—or should. We've suffered reverses here lately, and the—the outlook's not favorable.

HERBERT

Oh, things'll take a turn for the better!

MR. INCH

Well, it's uncertain, at best. November oats are up four points.

HERBERT

Ah, that's terrible, terrible—

MR. INCH

We are not rich in this girl's woods—I—I—mean vice versa—and my son's last dollar—a shining new silver dollar—it went into this cornerstone, with other mementos of the Age. —And the marble columns—we couldn't afford to buy them—they're dreadfully expensive—so—so—we just took them from the family vault in Mt. Hope. I don't think they'll mind—the people who are there, I mean.

HERBERT

[*Stoutly.*]
It's what they would wish, sir.

MR. INCH

—And finally there was the question of the bronze horse to settle—we planned to have one to put on top, you know, but—well—ever try to buy a bronze horse?

HERBERT

No, sir—I can't say I did.

MR. INCH

You've no idea what they come to—even used ones. So—so we had to fall back on the deer in our front yard. It had a lot of antlers and things but they unscrewed and we thought that maybe with it 'way high up there—

HERBERT

You'd never know it from a horse!

MR. INCH

Wouldn't you?

HERBERT

Never in this world!
   [MR. INCH *presses his arm gratefully.*]

MR. INCH

Herbert—

HERBERT

Yes, sir?

MR. INCH

Perhaps you'd like to stand with us, at the unveiling—

HERBERT

Me, sir?

MR. INCH

Yes.

HERBERT

Ah, 'twould be the crownin' glory of my life!

MR. INCH

Then we'll expect you here in ten minutes.
[*He moves Right.*]

HERBERT

I won't budge from the spot, sir!— And, oh,
thank you, thank you, sir!
[MR. INCH *goes out.* HERBERT *cracks his
whip.* KIT *enters up the steps from the
Boulevard.*]

KIT

Oh, Herbert—

HERBERT

Yes, sir? Where to, sir?

KIT

How long have you been here?

HERBERT

Mr. Canari, is it?— Quite awhile, sir.

KIT

Have you seen a young lady come up, in the last
few minutes?

HERBERT

[*Carefully.*]
On foot, would she be?

KIT

—In a car—a car with a Michigan license.

HERBERT

Nope—no Michigans to-day. [*Then cheerfully.*]
But she'll be along, sir. —And wouldn't she like a
nice carriage-ride, later on, when the moon comes
up? [KIT *is again examining the roped enclosure,
and does not answer.*] —Ummm—don't it smell
good, there on the river road. Ain't it still an' nice!
[*Still no answer from* KIT.] —Can't drive autos in
the Park, you know—City Ordinance.

KIT

Not this evening, thanks.
[HERBERT *smiles bravely.*]

HERBERT

As you like, sir.

KIT

If I were you, I'd keep off the Boulevard to-night.

HERBERT

Why's that?

KIT

It may be dangerous.

HERBERT

They can splutter all they like. They don't scare *us*, no more.

KIT

I'd get off it, and keep off.

HERBERT

Go hide in the Park, maybe. Cover ourselves with leaves, eh?

KIT

I particularly wouldn't go into the Park. I'd just go right home, stable my horse, and go to bed.

HERBERT

I guess *we're* all right.

KIT

Well, it's your own life.
[*A pause. Then a nervous pawing from below as a motor-car approaches with cut-out wide open.*]

HERBERT

This is our reg'lar stand. We stay put. [*But* JOSEPH *retires in a panic down the street.*] Hey! stop that horse! [*He runs down the steps. The*

*motor-car comes to a stop in the Boulevard below,
and* MARY's *voice is heard.*]

MARY

Kit?

KIT

Come on up! Quick! [MARY, *completely en-
veloped in a linen duster and a veil, mounts the
steps.*] Mary! [*He laughs.*] It *is* you, isn't it?
[*She removes the veil.*]

MARY

I've been driving since dawn. Fourteen hours.
Broke my back. *I* know the sight I am.

KIT

A sight for sore eyes, that's what you are.

MARY

Sweet Kit. —But don't mention eyes. Mine
won't focus. I see everything in the flat. Since
Buffalo I've gone down hill rapidly. Every mile-
stone I passed was a tombstone. Prop me up somewhere and tell me why you wired.

KIT

How does Spotless Town look to you?
[*She gazes at "The Elite."*]

MARY

There's the old Elite.   Anyway, *that's* the same.

KIT

Stung! It's the Elite Garage now. *My* Elite Garage. [*She stares. He nods.*] Nothing's the same, Mary.

MARY

I feel a thousand.

KIT

Except the Inches.   They remain constant.
[*A brief pause.*]

MARY

[*Lowly.*]
Why am I here, Kit? Why did you wire?

KIT

Have you had any dinner?

MARY

No—nor lunch—hadn't time. And I need food, Kit— I'm the sort that needs her food. And I could sleep, too— [*She slumps wearily against the wall.*] Oh, *I could sleep!*

KIT

You can eat and sleep to your heart's content, when it's over.

MARY

[*Impatiently.*]

When what's over? *What's* over—that's what I'm asking you.

KIT

I want you to wait and see for yourself.

MARY

Your voice sounds funny. I've a feeling I should have stayed in Detroit.

KIT

To keep on dying by degrees, eh?

[MARY *laughs shortly.*]

MARY

By inches, don't you mean?

KIT

Yes, that's just what I mean, Mary.

MARY

Tell me—tell me quickly—

[KIT *indicates the roped enclosure.*]

KIT

See that?

MARY

What's it for?

KIT

On that spot, in a few moments, there'll be something decided; whether Archie quits the horses, or whether he follows 'em to the end.

MARY

Then he's still at it—

KIT

Still at it. But look— [*She looks at him. He strikes* DR. MUNYON's *posture and raises a hopeful finger.*] "There is hope!" —You can save him. [MARY *starts and gasps.*]

MARY

Don't do that! [*She drops her face into her hands.*] I'm going dippy—

KIT

Um—for love of a man in a uniform—a white uniform. *I* know. Can't fool Kit.

MARY

But what can I do?

KIT

Wait and see what they're up to. Watch, and decide. Then if you want to stop it, I'm ready.

MARY

You didn't tell him I was coming—

KIT

Nope.

MARY

He's—never even asked for me?

KIT

Nope.

MARY

How—how does he seem?

KIT

Thin—and white. White as his uniform. They're
in a desperate state, Kiddo, desperate. You can't
dodge autos for ten hours a day, and— [MARY's
exclamation of pain cuts him short.] Sorry.

MARY

What holds him?— Is it just stubbornness, do
you think?

KIT

Deeper than that. Family stuff. Faith. [*A pause.*] Mary, in the front yard of that man's mind, there stands an iron deer. [MARY *laughs bitterly.*]

MARY

Deer? Oh, no! Horse!

KIT

Anyway, if you want to get it out, you've got to blast. To-night's the night. Now or never. Hence my telegram.

MARY

[*Thoughtfully.*]
—Got to blast.
[KIT *goes to the roped enclosure and takes two small rocks from the pile.*]

KIT

You'll see a ceremony here the like of which— well, I'll tell you just one thing about it: if it goes through, then at last the Inches' dream of glory is going to jell.

MARY

Jell?

KIT

Jell. Distill into a symbol. If you know Archie at all, you know that'll be the end of him.

MARY

But what can I do—? Oh, *Kit*—?
[KIT *returns to her with the rocks.*]

KIT

Just don't let it happen. Stop it. Here— [*He gives her the rocks.*] —If you think you need help, crock that arc-light— [*He points to the arc-light.*] —I'll be waiting in the garage for the signal—got my troops all lined up— [*He consults a slip of paper.*] —Nine Ramblers, eleven Stanley-Steamers, six Pope-Toledos, eight Wintons, three Americans—

MARY

That's plenty, plenty—

KIT

They'll pour out down below there, close ranks, and charge up around into the Parkway, along here into the Park. Once I turn 'em loose, nothing can stop 'em. They'll smash this to bits, Mary—what's left, Archie can put into his hat. So there you are— You press the button and I'll do the rest.

[MARY *glances off Left.*]

MARY

The arc-light—

KIT

Just keep plugging till you hit it.

MARY

I won't miss but once— Then throw myself at his head, eh?

[KIT *grins.*]

KIT

Sure!— And rebound, maybe. [*A brief pause.*] —I'll catch you if you do, Mary. [*She looks at him. He grins again.*]

MARY

Kit, you fool, you.

KIT

There should have been two of you, you know. One for me.

MARY

Oh, I *like* you so *much*. *Twice* as much as him.

KIT

"But"—?

[MARY *gestures helplessly.*]

MARY

But.

KIT

That's all right. I have my stamp-collection.
[*There is a noise of some one coming from off Right.
He draws her into the shadows.*] Here they are.
—I warn you now. They'll just about break your
heart. Mind you don't get touched, and go soft.
He's a drowning man—may struggle—brutal, kiddo,
be brutal!

MARY

—Iron deer—got to blast—

KIT

—White Wings' last stand—your last chance.
Well—don't cry on your dynamite.

[*He goes out, down the steps to the Boulevard.
MARY leans back against the wall, and places
the two rocks within reach at her side. A
moment of silence, then ARCHIE hurries in
from Right, carrying a folded American flag,
which he places on the foundation without
unfolding it. Nervously, furtively, he
examines the structure to see that everything
is ready. He wears his White Wing uniform,
and his face is nearly as white as it. MARY
watches him for a moment, then steps out of*

the shadow, and faces him. At the sound of
her footstep, he turns and sees her. For an
instant their eyes hold them rigid, speechless.
Then, all at once, they rush together, and
MARY *buries herself in his arms, with a cry.*]

MARY

Archie!

ARCHIE

You've *come*—

MARY

Tight, you—*tight!* Oh, break my back—*break* it!
[*They kiss.*]

ARCHIE

Dear, oh, my dear—
[*She stands off from him a little, and runs her*
hand up and down the front of his jacket.]

MARY

You're thin. You're so thin. Poor, poor darling
—what have they done to you?

ARCHIE

Awful—it's been awful.

MARY

I know! All day long— [*In recitative.*] —Nine

Ramblers, 'leven Stanley-Steamers, six Pope-Toledos—

[ARCHIE *lowers his head and begins to dodge.*]

ARCHIE

[*Agonized.*]
Don't—don't—
[MARY *gathers him into her arms.*]

MARY

Never mind—never mind.   —Mary's with you,
Archie—

ARCHIE

You had to come—you missed me so—

MARY

I won't miss but once.

ARCHIE

It's as good as a mile.

MARY

It's a sight for sore eyes.   —Dippy, I am—quite
dippy.   —You're so white.

ARCHIE

White's my color.

MARY

—Spotless of Spotless Town. Oh, I'm in love with
a man in a uniform, me—you press the button, I'll
do the rest—

[*He draws her closer to him.*]

ARCHIE

Mary—

MARY

Listen, Archie Inch: years are inches. Year by
year we die by inches, inch by inch, year by year—

ARCHIE

Then let's together—it takes longer.

MARY

I don't know, I don't know.

ARCHIE

Marry me, Mary.

MARY

—He said you were a drowning man, Kit did—are
you drowned, my dear?

ARCHIE

[*Wretchedly.*]
I don't know what I am.

MARY

You're a White Wing.

[ARCHIE *attempts to lift his head proudly.*]

ARCHIE

A White Wing!

MARY

[*Bitterly.*]

Horse-power, that's what—and stalled dead.

ARCHIE

Then start me—start me.

MARY

Look, Archie— [*She raises her finger:* DOCTOR
MUNYON *in the poster.*] "I can save you!"
—You'll start—I can start you! [*She works his
arms once, with a cranking motion, then puts her
mouth against his.*] Breathe again—breathe— I'll
prime you—breathe—*breathe!*

ARCHIE

Oh, marry me, Mary—marry me!

MARY

[*Against his breast.*]

—And you'll quit 'em, you'll quit 'em, won't you—

ARCHIE

What?

MARY

—The horses, quit the horses.

ARCHIE

How could I, dear?

MARY

Easy! Easy!

ARCHIE

But they're beautiful—you don't know! All our
traditions, our—

MARY

No more of that! Hear me? [*A motor-car roars
past in the Boulevard.*] There's *our* music!
    [*In a blind fury* ARCHIE *wheels about from her
    in the direction of the noise.*]

ARCHIE

Bastards! We'll fix 'em—*we'll* show *them,* we
will! [*Then, in a careful, plotting voice*]: —To-
night, Mary—great event—my last dollar goes into
it—make history—history! See here—Construction on Eastern Parkway—Major Philip Inch Dedi-
cates—"Old Things Are Best," says Archie Inch in
Special Interview.

MARY

New things are best!

ARCHIE

—Something old, something new—oh, *when* will
you marry me, Mary?

MARY

When will you quit 'em?

ARCHIE

I can't—ever—

MARY

Then watch out—I'll rebound! [*She flings herself against him. He stands firm. She drops her
face into her hands, murmuring:*] —Dippy, quite
dippy—oh, catch me, catch me, some one! [*From off
Right comes the murmur of voices and the sound of
wheels. She looks up, suddenly.*] What's that?

ARCHIE

It's my family.

MARY

[*Sharply.*]
And it's me!

ARCHIE

But they're old—

MARY

—And I'm new!—I'm new and bright and shiny! [*She faces him with her hands out, offering herself, asking him to choose.*] Well?

ARCHIE

Dear, there are some things—once they're explained to you—

MARY

"Explained"!?— Oh, my poor boy— [*A brief pause.*] —It's true, then, I've got to blast.
[*The sound from off Right draws nearer.*]

ARCHIE

After this ceremony's over, I'll— [CLYDE SIMS *comes in, Right, in White Wing uniform. On a wheel-barrow in front of him he wheels a large object loosely covered with a strip of burlap.* ARCHIE *points to the shadows, back Left.*] —Wait a moment back there—it won't take long.

CLYDE

All ready, Archie—here they come.
[*He stops the wheel-barrow near the foundation, removes the burlap and reveals a battered and rusty iron deer. He and* ARCHIE *lift it from the wheel-barrow, set it in place on top of the foundation and cover it with*

the old American flag. A procession begins to enter from Right. First come two men, DR. BOWLES and DR. DERBY, the one in clerical garb, with Roman collar, the other in cap and gown. Their faces are expressionless as masks. CLYDE gives them programs for the ceremony.]

DR. DERBY

[*To* DR. BOWLES.]
These affairs are always late.
[DR. BOWLES *consults his watch.*]

DR. BOWLES

Shocking!

DR. DERBY

I know this costume's not suitable for the evening, but I've been so busy all day with meetings and what-not—you understand?

DR. BOWLES

Trust in God and no one will notice.
[MR. INCH *comes in and greets them quietly. Following him, in an invalid-chair made from a segment of one of the little red carts, comes the old Major, in full White Wing dress-uniform, with Decorations. The chair is propelled by* MRS. INCH, *now of the shabby-*

genteel. HERBERT *comes last, carrying his hat. All receive programs from* CLYDE *and group themselves near the foundation.* MR. INCH *whispers to* MRS. INCH:]

MR. INCH

I think I'm against this—it's been so dreadfully expensive, and— [MRS. INCH *glares at him.*] I've got a right to my opinion, Fanny.

ARCHIE

Are you ready, Dr. Bowles?
[DR. BOWLES *nods, advances and bows his head. All become quiet and all heads are bowed. With great unction, and a marked clerical intonation,* DR. BOWLES *begins:*]

DR. BOWLES

Jabber, jabber, jabber, jab—jabber, jabber. Jabber, jabber, jabber, jab, jab, jabberjab. [*He takes a long breath.*] Jaaaaaaaaber, jab, jabber. Jaaaaber jab—jabber. [*And concludes very impressively:*] Jabber, jabber, jabber.
[*All respond in chorus.*]

ALL

Jabber.
[*All raise their heads again.* DR. BOWLES *retires.*]

ARCHIE

The speech of acceptance is to be made by a gentleman whose reputation is known to us all: Dr. Derby —Horace Peabody Proctor Professor of Veterinary Science and Associated Arts and Crafts. **Dr. Derby**!

[*He bows to* DR. DERBY, *who advances pompously.*]

MR. INCH

[*To* MRS. INCH, *in a whisper.*]
Isn't it in the wrong order?
[*She shakes her head vigorously.*]

MRS. INCH

Hush!

MR. INCH

—But something must have upset Archie. Archie— [ARCHIE *looks at him.*] —Upset?
[ARCHIE *shakes his head.* DR. DERBY *clears his throat.*]

DR. DERBY

Good evening all— The subject of my address was to be "Has the Horse a Soul, Like Myself"— Has he a soul?— But the fact is I hadn't time to prepare it. So I can merely thank you from— [*All find places and seat themselves. He proceeds.*] —My heart, Mr.—er—Inch—

MRS. INCH

[*Whispering.*]
—*Major* Inch.

DR. DERBY

—*Major* Inch—for myself, for the City, for the University, and for all lovers of the Horse, whose name is Legion.— I may say that the conclusion of my address was to be "Indeed He Has!"

[*He bows. All applaud. He retires.*]

ARCHIE

Now I have the honor to present Major Philip E. Inch, who will preside over the formal unveiling of the Major Philip E. Inch Memorial White Marble Drinking Fountain for Horses—

[*Assisted by* MR. *and* MRS. INCH, MAJOR INCH *rises.*]

MAJOR INCH

It is nothing. As a young man with General Boocock, I was wounded in the service of the horse. In that instant I foresaw his future and determined to found a family which would follow him to the end. But I take to myself no credit whatsoever for the Major Philip E. Inch Memorial White Marble Drinking-Fountain for Horses—the idea originated with my grandson Archibald, upon whose shoulders now rests the entire burden of our tradition—

MARY

[From the shadows.]
—And what a load.

DR. BOWLES

Quiet there, please.

MARY

After you, Alphonse.

DR. DERBY

Look out now, I have influence.

MARY

I've had it.

DR. DERBY

I mean I can have you arrested.

MARY

Chestnuts.

MRS. INCH

Plainly a case of the wrong training in childhood.

MARY

Chestnuts. Horse chestnuts.

ARCHIE

Go on, Grandfather.

MAJOR INCH

—My grandson conceived this Fountain as a means of shaming speed-demons into the abandonment of their fiendish engines for return to the great God-given means of conveyance, Holy Horse. [*All, except* MARY, *uncover,* MRS. INCH *unpinning her hat. The* MAJOR *proceeds:*] —For our destinies are welded—Horse and Inch, Inch and Horse. The motor-car is our common enemy—it attacks all our time-honored customs and traditions—

MARY

If they can't stand, let them fall!

MAJOR INCH

Ernest, speak to the woman.

MR. INCH

[*To* MARY.]
How do you do?

MRS. INCH

Speak to her!

MR. INCH

I did.

ARCHIE

Go on, Grandfather!

MAJOR INCH

—While we recognize the motor-car as the merest passing fad, the aim and purpose of the Major Philip E. Inch Memorial White Marble—

MARY

—Monument to the horse!

ARCHIE

Mary!

MARY

A fountain?— Soon there won't be a horse left to drink from it!

ARCHIE

Mary!

MRS. INCH

You know this person?

MARY

Can seven people hold the world back with a water-trough? Can they, Archie? Oh, *make* it a monument, do!— And top it with a Winged Defeat, for children of old White Wings to come and weep at.

MAJOR INCH

She-devil! Slut! Take her off!

MARY

Yes—and move it to one side—quick!—it's blocking traffic!

MRS. INCH

Who is this woman?

ARCHIE

I'm sure I don't know.

MARY

You—? [*She closes her eyes, sways slightly, makes a half-gesture toward him and murmurs:*] Oh—

ARCHIE

Go on, Grandfather!

[*The MAJOR gathers himself to proceed. Suddenly MARY takes a stone from the wall and throws it at the arc-light. It misses. The MAJOR proceeds:*]

MAJOR INCH

Beneath the accusing finger of this white marble edifice, the roaring, shrieking, crazy rush will cease. . . . [MARY *throws another stone with more deliberation. There is a crash, and the sound of shattered glass as the arc-light is extinguished. All start in alarm, but the MAJOR plunges on:*] Fare-

well, this Juggernaut hell-bent on destruction—
[*From the garage below, in swelling volume, comes
the sound of many motors starting. He raises his
voice.*] Welcome again, peace and tranquillity. . . .
[*He turns right.*] Stop that noise!— Welcome,
quiet streets, calm countryside— [*His voice cracks.
He wheels savagely about, mounts his wheel-chair
and calls over the wall:*] Have that noise stopped,
I say! Have it stopped! [*The noise continues. He
gathers himself for a final shriek.*] Have it stopped
or—or I withdraw my gift!

> [*The noise grows louder.* MAJOR INCH *draws
> himself up threateningly, then all at once
> crumples into his chair.* ARCHIE *and* MRS.
> INCH *fly to him. The noise of the motors has
> become a steady, low roar.*]

MR. INCH

Maybe—maybe we'd better go home.

> [MRS. INCH *begins to trundle the* MAJOR *off,
> Right.* MR. INCH *and the others follow.*
> ARCHIE *and* MARY *are left alone. The door
> of the garage is opened, the noise of the
> motor-cars increases for a moment, then di-
> minishes into a steady roaring bass as they
> pass along the Boulevard. Gradually, to this
> bass, bulb horns add a treble in minor key,
> similar to the opening phrase of "White
> Wings, They Never Grow Weary."*]

MARY

Archie—

ARCHIE

This—all of this—it's what *you* stand for, is it?

MARY

All of it!

ARCHIE

Noise and speed. . . .

MARY

Music! Flight!
  [ARCHIE *turns from her.*]

ARCHIE

Agh!

MARY

Oh, they caught you young— Devils! Grew whiskers on *you* in the cradle, poor dear. . . .

ARCHIE

God, this racket!
  [*Their voices begin to synchronize with the beat of the motors.*]

MARY

Archie—you hear the world move—you'll move with it!

ARCHIE

I've heard Grandfather's heart crack in two— I've heard *that*—

MARY

But Grandpa's day's done. He's *had* his day, Grandpa. Move, Archie—*move!* Else you'll rot on your feet.

ARCHIE

Move?

MARY

Quit the horses!

ARCHIE

Not so long as I live!

MARY

Live? Die! That's all history—finished!

ARCHIE

They're my life—I'm a White Wing!
[*She takes him by the arms and wheels him
   about into the light, searching his face for
   some ray of hope.*]

MARY

Deep roots, iron deer have. [*She clings to him suddenly, desperately.*] Oh, *Archie*—help me save you!

> [*The noise of the motors falls into a faster staccato, of definite pattern. Their voices coincide in speed and emphasis.*]

ARCHIE

You're not for me. I see that. [*With a gesture.*] Better go. I stay put.

MARY

But we *love*—you and me— We two *love!* What of that?

ARCHIE

Go! I don't want to see you! I'm through with you! Go!

MARY

[*Rapidly.*]

Quit, quit, quit, quit, quit—quit the horses, quit the horses—

ARCHIE

[*More rapidly still.*]

Go! I don't want you! I'm through with you! Go!

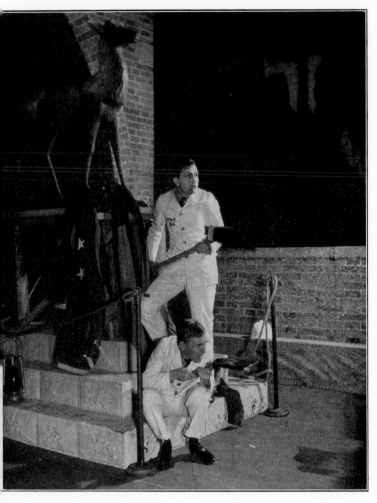

SCENE FROM ACT II, SCENE 2

[MARY *strains against him, her face lifted to his.*]

MARY

Quit! Will you quit? Will you quit? Will you quit?

ARCHIE

No! Never! Will you go? Will you *go?*
[*She drags his hand to her lips and kisses it.*]

MARY

[*Sobbing.*]
Good-bye, Archie boy—
[ARCHIE *looks away, his face contorted.*]

ARCHIE

Good-bye—good-*bye*—

MARY

[*Through her tears.*]
Mind your step in the street. Cars come quick.
Don't get hit.
[*He shakes his head, unable to speak. The motors are still racing past in a steady stream below. The different-toned bulb horns keep reiterating in minor key variations on the eight notes of the opening phrase of "White Wings, They Never Grow Weary."*]

[MARY *goes swiftly to the steps, and out. A*
moment, then CLYDE *comes running on from*
Left, a white streak through the darkness.]

CLYDE

[*Gasping.*]

Archie! They're turning up here! Headed for
the Park! The Park—Archie! Get out of the way!
Driving like demons—knock the Fountain to bits!
[*He tries to drag* ARCHIE *off Right.*] Come on—
quick!

ARCHIE

No!

[CLYDE *runs out.* MR. INCH *hurries in from*
Left, glancing fearfully back over his shoul-
der. He is frightened out of his wits.]

MR. INCH

Archie! Look out, Son. Get out of here!

[ARCHIE *seizes his father's wrist and brings*
him to one of the little red carts. He un-
covers it and takes the shovel and broom
from it. MR. INCH *looks at* ARCHIE *in de-*
spair. ARCHIE *holds the shovel out to him.*]

MR. INCH

[*In a panic.*]

But why, Archie, why?

[Archie *thrusts the shovel into* Mr. Inch's *trembling hands and himself takes the broom. A faint light from the distant approaching headlights begins to play over the monument.* Archie *leads* Mr. Inch *to the foundation, and they mount it together. The sound of the approaching motors again swells into a roaring bass for the shrill treble of the horns' insistent phrase.* Archie *whips the flag off the iron deer. The headlights now blaze from off Left, and break over the two figures upon the monument.*

ARCHIE

—For the Horse, Father!

[Archie *stiffens and faces the onrushing motors, broom upraised in one hand, while the other supports his drooping father.*]

CURTAIN

WHITE WINGS : ACT THREE

ACT III

The Parkway at dawn on a winter morning, several years later. The city has prospered. There is now an office-building several stories high in the background, and a higher one under construction near it. The pattern of clouds, however, is unchanged.

The foundation for the Memorial Drinking-Fountain has been removed. Against the wall at Left stands a green park-bench. In the Boulevard below stand JOSEPH and the cab, but HERBERT is absent from the box. At Right, against the Parkway curb, stands a small galvanized-iron can, and near it, in the old position, one sadly dilapidated little red cart. Occasionally in the course of the act, motor-cars are heard passing in the Boulevard.

The sparrows are chattering noisily and MR. INCH, who appears to have aged considerably, is seated upon the bench at back, poring over a notebook. He wears a rusty black overcoat over his white uniform. Bright light still comes from elec-

tric street-lamps, off Left and Right. For a mo-
ment MR. INCH *stares moodily into space, biting*
his lip. Gradually his hand steals into his coat-
pocket and brings forth a large revolver, of the
sort known as "horse-pistol." He holds it away
from him, his hand trembling while he once more
hopelessly examines the note-book. Gradually, re-
luctantly, his eyes turn to the pistol. He gasps
and shudders. Then he takes a deep breath, rises
and places the barrel of the pistol against his
stomach, waits an instant, looks down at it, then
shakes his head, and puts it into his mouth. He
removes it with a grimace and spits disgustedly
into his cart. Then he seats himself upon the
bench, reverses his hold upon the weapon so that
his thumb is upon the trigger, and presses the
barrel against his helmet. His poor little face
wrinkles in horrible anticipation. Suddenly from
the Boulevard below comes a sharp whinny, from
JOSEPH, *the Horse.* MR. INCH's *hand closes con-*
vulsively, and the pistol slips up against his hel-
met and is discharged. From above a dead spar-
row drops at MR. INCH's *feet. He picks it up,*
regards it in bewilderment, murmurs "A sparrow"
and chucks it into his cart. A step is heard from
off Right. MR. INCH *glances anxiously in that*
direction, then quickly hides the pistol beneath his
helmet upon the bench, reseats himself upon the
curbstone and begins once more to pore over the

note-book. ARCHIE, *dragging his broom behind
him, enters from Right, in uniform, with a mourn-
ing-band about his sleeve. He, too, appears older,
and there are bitter lines about his eyes and
mouth. He stops, and looks suspiciously at* MR.
INCH.

ARCHIE

I thought I heard a report.

MR. INCH

There—there wasn't a bit of truth in it.

ARCHIE

I smell smoke.

MR. INCH

That factory's burning soft coal, on the sly.
   [ARCHIE *goes to his side.*]

ARCHIE

There's a hole in your hat.

MR. INCH

A—a moth got into it. [*Pettishly.*] Can't a moth
get into a man's hat without all these questions?
   [ARCHIE *indicates the note-book.*]

ARCHIE

What's that?

MR. INCH

It's awful—last month's accounts.

ARCHIE

As bad as ever?

MR. INCH

Worse. [ARCHIE *seats himself beside him.*] Just listen, Archie: "Rent, for one nasty little drafty bedroom for A. Inch, E. Inch and Major P. E. Inch, eighteen dollars; very indifferent food, thirty-one dollars; laundry, nineteen-twenty-five; final installment undertaker's bill, interment Mrs. Fanny K. Inch, fifty-four-forty—

ARCHIE

That pomp was ridiculous.

MR. INCH

No pomp was too ridiculous for Fanny. —Oh, and Archie—what *can* we do about Grandpa's goings-on?

ARCHIE

Poor old fellow.

MR. INCH

But it's such an item: "Fine, Major Inch, va-
grancy, ten dollars; fine, Major Inch, sassing traffic-
cop, five dollars; fine, Major Inch, committing nui-
sance in Packard salesrooms, twenty dollars—"
Where's it coming from? Where's it coming from?

ARCHIE

Lord only knows.

MR. INCH

—Then there were all sorts of divers sundries,
what-nots and unaccounted-fors—and when I got all
through I had to spend another ten cents for red
ink, to write down the deficit.

ARCHIE

I'll keep the accounts after this.

MR. INCH

I wish you would! Well—I suppose we'd ought
to get started again.

ARCHIE

It isn't four yet. Let's wait till the café crowd
goes home.

MR. INCH

This night work'll kill me some day—Or some

night. I miss my sleep. Sleep's nice. I *like* to
sleep— [*A pause.*] —It's lonely, Archie—just
the two of us left, this way.

ARCHIE

Two?

MR. INCH

Of the *real* ones, I mean. [*He sniffs contemptuously.*] They *call* themselves White Wings.

ARCHIE

There are hose-men enough.
[MR. INCH *sniffs again.*]

MR. INCH

Hose-men!

ARCHIE

Oh, don't play the snob! It only makes us more
ridiculous than we are.

MR. INCH

You can say what you like—it *hasn't* the quality
of the old handwork.

ARCHIE

Damn the quality.

MR. INCH

What I *don't* see, is where the City gets the right to expect us to help with the ashes.

ARCHIE

Don't you? Well, take my word for it, it'll be garbage next.
  [*He kicks the galvanized can by way of empha-
    sis.* MR. INCH *rises.*]

MR. INCH

When that comes, I quit!

ARCHIE

Come along—
  [MR. INCH *turns suddenly and grasps his arm.*]

MR. INCH

Son, why don't you get out of it?

ARCHIE

You know why. [*With intense hate.*] Mother—
she knows why, too!

MR. INCH

You've turned bitter, Son.

ARCHIE

Have I?

MR. INCH

I—I don't believe in death-bed promises. She oughtn't to have asked it.

ARCHIE

But she did, didn't she? And I promised.

MR. INCH

Break it!

ARCHIE

You didn't teach me to break promises, as a child. You taught me to keep them, regardless. [*With sudden venom.*] Oh, you taught me a lot of fine things!

MR. INCH

—"So long as there's a horse left in town—" That was like Fanny. She was a great girl for plugging loopholes. [*A pause. Then softly, insinuatingly.*] —But maybe—maybe if there were a few more fires like last night's at Potts' Livery Stables—if a few of them were to happen *together*, say—

ARCHIE

Don't talk rot, Father. Come on—
　　[*He moves Left.*]

MR. INCH

Archie, you'd ought to have married that nice crazy Todd girl.

ARCHIE

Let's get going, shall we?

MR. INCH

I—I wrote her a letter, the other day.

ARCHIE

You—? [*Sharply.*] What do you mean?!

MR. INCH

It—it was just a friendly sort of letter: "H-how are you?" and "Hope your father's still doing well," and—and—well, I had some ink left over, and—

ARCHIE

Take your cart and come along. [MR. INCH *makes a half-hearted attempt to push his cart into action.*] Come along, old fellow.

MR. INCH

I—just—can't. I can't do it to-night. Don't ask me to go on again to-night. I'm tired, Son.
   [*He goes back to the bench and sinks down upon it.*]

ARCHIE

Oh, I know!

MR. INCH

No, you don't. No one knows. Forty-two years I've been at it, Archie. Forty-two years—

ARCHIE

Come on, old chap. —That won't help any.

MR. INCH

—From eight in the morning till six at night—every day—sweep and shovel, shovel and sweep. And now, these last two years, from midnight till seven, shovel and sweep, sweep and shovel. I can't go on any longer, Archie.

[*He begins to cry softly. Archie comforts him.*]

ARCHIE

There, there, old man—never mind. We'll arrange something for you.

MR. INCH

F-f-forty-two years I've been at it. I've done my best—no one can say I haven't done my best. I've been gay—I've whistled at my work— [*He makes a pitiful attempt to whistle now.*] —But I can't

TAXI-DRIVER, *himself a most urbane gentle-*
man in an immaculate uniform, leaps to the
pavement and opens the door for MARY *to*
alight. She is smartly dressed in a modern
suit of some dark material, but otherwise
appears to have changed very little.]

MARY

One moment, please— [*She goes to the end of*
the Parkway wall, Right, and calls down into the
street.] Hello, there!

[*The garage window is opened.*]

A VOICE

Canari Motor Works. Night Watchman speaking.

MARY

Is Mr. Kit Canari there?

THE VOICE

Who is it wants him, please?

MARY

Miss Todd—Mary Todd.

THE VOICE

Afraid I can't disturb him now. He's in bed.

MARY

Then get him up. It's important! [*She returns to the* TAXI-DRIVER.] How much?

TAXI-DRIVER

Two hundred and twenty-nine seventy.

MARY

That's a lot.

TAXI-DRIVER

It's my regular rate, Miss. Quite a run from Detroit, you know. Still, if you feel it's exorbitant—

MARY

Oh, no—that's for you to decide.

TAXI-DRIVER

—Or the taximeter, let us say!

MARY

I beg your pardon.

TAXI-DRIVER

Not at all.

MARY

Here you are—that's two hundred and fifty.

TAXI-DRIVER

Thanks loads. And a thousand apologies for those annoying brake-bands.

MARY

Not at all—how much is the car itself worth?

TAXI-DRIVER

—To sell, you mean?

MARY

[*Quickly.*]
Would you sell it?

TAXI-DRIVER

With pleasure, if you'd care to have it. —Shall we say a hundred and fifty?

MARY

I'll take it for that.

TAXI-DRIVER

Splendid! Let me see now; a hundred and fifty from two fifty—one hundred dollars.

[*He returns a number of the bills she has given him.*]

MARY

Thank you.

TAXI-DRIVER

Thank *you.*
   [*He goes to the cab and returns with a walking-stick.*]

MARY

Good-bye.
   [*He smiles, engagingly.*]

TAXI-DRIVER

Let us say "Au revoir"?

MARY

All right.

TAXI-DRIVER

Au revoir.

MARY

Au revoir.
   [*He smiles, doffs his cap, bows slightly and goes off, Right, in the direction of Detroit, contentedly swinging his stick.* KIT *comes up the steps from the Boulevard.*]

KIT

Mary—is it really you?
   [*She laughs.*]

MARY

So far as I know, Kit.
[*He goes to her quickly.*]

KIT

May I?

MARY

Will you?
[*She puts her face up. He kisses her hand.*]

KIT

But you said you'd never come back.

MARY

That was silly of me.

KIT

Tell me what brought you.

MARY

The Rolls, there— [*She takes a letter from her bag.*] —And this. Listen—it's from Archie's father: [*She reads the letter.*] "Dear Miss Mary Todd: Well, how are things going with you? Things are not going so well here. I wish you could do something about my boy Archie. We're obliged now to live three in one room and we go to bed at

8 A.M., but all morning long he keeps calling in his sleep 'Mary! Mary! Oh, Mary! Mary! Mary!' And it is really rather difficult for me, as I work hard all night, am nearly sixty-three, and need my rest. I am afraid that it is a matter of life or death, possibly both, and trust that you will take immediate steps, and no joke about it. Well, good-bye for the present, from your friend and well-wisher, Ernest Inch." [*She returns the letter to her bag.*] —And it's in red ink.

KIT

What about it?

MARY

I've come to marry him, Kit.

KIT

Are you crazy?

MARY

Probably.

KIT

—Still really in *love* with him?

MARY

I want to kiss him.

KIT

Then do, for God's sake, and get it over with.

MARY

I did—but it didn't. I keep on wanting to.

KIT

—So because a woman wants to kiss a man, she marries him!

MARY

Do you know a better reason?

KIT

Pardon me, while I get out my ear-trumpet.

MARY

I'm wiser than you in lots of ways, old son. I've learned that some things don't change.

KIT

—And Archie's job is one of them.

MARY

No—I've come to take him away from it.

KIT

What if he won't go?
    [MARY *smiles.*]

MARY

In that case, I may have to marry you, after all.

KIT

Do you mean it?

MARY

Yes, if you like. [*A brief pause.*] You're sweet, Kit—and long-suffering. [*With decision.*] Yes, if you like!

KIT

Careful!— You'll never marry Archie—never in this world. It's too crazy.

[*She moves Right.*]

MARY

—I'll look for him along here. You wait.

KIT

—I've told you, Mary: the Inches will follow 'em so long as there's one left to follow.

[MARY *stops and turns.*]

MARY

—You might find out, if you can, just how many there *are* left to follow.

[*She goes out.* KIT *mounts the bench to look over the wall, stepping on the revolver as he*

does so. He picks it up in surprise, and ex-
amines it.]

HERBERT

[*Opening his eyes again.*]
—That wouldn't be hard to answer, sir.
[KIT *hastily puts the pistol in his pocket and*
turns in surprise.]

KIT

What wouldn't?

HERBERT

—"How many horses."

KIT

You haven't been listening, or anything like that,
have you?

HERBERT

What else've I got to do, I'd like to know?

KIT

Maybe *you* agree with me that the Inches will stay
at it till they die—

HERBERT

Well—Mr. *Archie's* apt to. Promised his ma—
that so long's there's a plug left in town—

KIT

[*Quickly.*]
Are you sure of that?

HERBERT

—Heard 'im say so with 'is own lips. [*He chuckles.*] —Touchin', ain't it? But as for that question of your lady friend's—

KIT

Well, what about it?

HERBERT

[*Cautiously.*]
—How many left—just at this moment?

KIT

Yes.

HERBERT

An.

KIT

What's that?

HERBERT

An horse. —This half-paralyzed ruin 'at stands before you now.

KIT

You're talking through your hat.

HERBERT

Oh, I am, am I?   Listen here, Mister: I don't doubt but there'll always be horses in the provincial cities—I suppose you can find a number of 'em right this minute in such places as N'York an' Boston. But please to remember that this town *makes* autos. Ain't been a *private*-owned horse here since Mrs. Prentice's bays went under the hammer to George Major, in Amityville.

KIT

There are plenty of others.

HERBERT

Yeah-ah?   Well, last September, the Quality Dairy moved out to Brighton. On January first, the Upton Chain stores went on a strictly cash-an'-carry basis.   An' so on an' so forth till last night, when Potts' Livery burned to the ground.   All was lost except Josie: he got out down a fire-escape. —So when I say "an horse left" I mean *an horse left*—   Don't I, Josie?

    [*The horse whinnies asthmatically.*]

KIT

But confound it, this is serious! How old is the brute?

HERBERT

Mister, you wouldn't believe me. I might tell you he was born the same day as old Major Inch—but what's the use?

[*A short, strangled whinny from Josie.*]

KIT

I don't like the sound of that throat. —And paralyzed too, you say?

HERBERT

Sure! Practically completely paralyzed. But he don't mind. It's the charley-horses he minds. He suffers terrible with charley-horses.

[*A heart-rending whinny from* JOSIE. KIT
becomes more nervous.]

KIT

May prove too much for him at almost any time, eh?

HERBERT

Oh, don't you worry your head over Josie!

KIT

—But I'm agonized over Josie! —If there weren't any horses, how could there be White Wings?

HERBERT

There couldn't. —Not the genuine.

KIT

Archie'd be let out in spite of himself—well, he mustn't be!

HERBERT

He won't, sir— Joseph here—he's good for years yet.

KIT

I wouldn't give him five minutes, in a fog. Listen, Herbert—

HERBERT

Yes, sir?

KIT

Archie's job is as important to me as to him, now. So you and I have got to arrange somehow to have at least three horses kept in the city right along, day and night. Do you know any one with any, in the country hereabouts?

HERBERT

Well, there's my Aunt Eunice. She keeps a string o' polo ponies out near Honeoye.

[KIT *hurries down the steps and out into the Boulevard.*]

KIT'S VOICE

Take me to the Western Union.

HERBERT

Sure. —But don't you give yourself one moment's concern over Josie.

KIT'S VOICE

Get a move on, will you?

HERBERT

Clllck! Clllck! [*His head and shoulders are seen to turn slowly, and the sound of slow wheels and faltering hoof-beats is heard as they move off Right.*] —Joseph lives a sort of charmed life, might say. Why, Mister, sometimes I think this horse is immortal. You'd be surprised if I was to tell you the real name o' the winner o' the Kentucky Derby back in '84— Yes, sir! Why, you wouldn't believe me! Cllck—cllck!— Take it easy, Josie—

[*The Parkway is empty for a moment, then* MAJOR INCH *steals on from Left, shrunken and dishevelled in an old Union uniform and*

*campaign hat. In his hand he carries a small
tack-hammer. He looks about him furtively,
then takes two pins from his coat-lapel,
crouches down beside the taxi-cab and drives
them into a rear tire. This done, he rises
again and peers down the Parkway, Left,
where he spies another quarry. His old eyes
light up expectantly, he takes another pin
from his lapel, raises his hammer and runs
stealthily off Right.* MARY *reënters slowly
up the steps, goes to the bench, and gazes
moodily down the street.* ARCHIE *enters
from Left, goes to the cart, and places his
broom in it.* MARY *senses rather than sees
him. They turn simultaneously and meet
each other's eyes.*]

MARY

[*In a whisper.*]
Archie— [*He stares at her, speechless.*]   Hello,
Archie.

ARCHIE

[*Without moving.*]
Hello, Mary.

MARY

"Hello-hello"—is that all?

ARCHIE

What else?

MARY

There must be a thousand things.

ARCHIE

I don't know them. [*For another moment they gaze at each other, transfixed, then, he turns his cart about.*] If you'll excuse me—I must go to work.

MARY

No!

ARCHIE

I'm sorry. It's been—nice to see you.
[*He begins slowly to wheel the cart off Right.*]

MARY

Oh, my dear—you're lame—
[ARCHIE *laughs harshly.*]

ARCHIE

So I am.

MARY

How did it happen?

ARCHIE

—I was trying to hold the world back, if you'll remember. [*He laughs again.*] —It rolled over on my foot. [*With an exclamation, she starts toward him.*] Stay where you are, Mary! [*She stops dead. A pause. Then:*] Now, listen: It's no use. I'm a White Wing. I was born one. I'll die one.

MARY

I don't care!

ARCHIE

[*Ironically.*]
You'd like to share my brilliant life?— Join me in the Gentle Art of Sweeping Up?

MARY

[*Eagerly.*]
—That's—that's all you call it now?

ARCHIE

I call it manure. [*His voice rises.*] I call most things manure!

MARY

[*Softly.*]
The great Inch tradition—

ARCHIE

Manure.

MARY

The faith of your fathers—

ARCHIE

Manure.

MARY

[*Sharply.*]
Then get out of it!

ARCHIE

Why?
[*She looks at him a moment.   Then falters.*]

MARY

Love—

ARCHIE

Manure.   [*She gasps, stiffens, then goes to him swiftly and strikes him across the face with her open hand.   He seizes her wrists and drags her against him.*]   You—!   [*For a moment they stand rigid, glaring savagely at one another.   Then all at once she slumps into his arms.*]

MARY

Oh, marry me—

ARCHIE

No.

MARY

Marry me, Archie—marry me!

ARCHIE

I can't.

MARY

Come with me, Archie—come, dear—we'll go—
[*He shakes his head.*] I've bought you a taxi-cab—
see? I'll teach you to run it.

ARCHIE

I must stay as I am.

MARY

Now—? When you know what it is? When you
feel as you do?

ARCHIE

I can't help myself. [*She stands off from him and
looks at him, uncomprehendingly.*] I promised my
mother on her death-bed.

MARY

But the dead can't hold the living!

ARCHIE

Oh—*can't* they!

MARY

It's wicked! It's sinful!

ARCHIE

It was part of the scheme for me.

MARY

—A promise like that—

ARCHIE

A promise is a promise.

MARY

Oh, my poor boy—

ARCHIE

—And I'll keep it. There's always some one who gets caught between two ages. I'll keep it—it will round out my life. Good-bye— [*He gropes for her.*] Darling—darling—

MARY

No, no! I don't! I'm sick of saying good-bye to you!

ARCHIE

We're not for each other. Good-bye, dear— good-bye.

MARY

Oh, I love you!

ARCHIE

—And I you.

MARY

Come with me.

ARCHIE

Good-bye—

MARY

[*Wildly.*]

Then I'll stay! We'll face it out together. I'll put starch in your uniforms. I'll keep your shoes shined bright!

> [*The cab returns to its stand in the Boulevard. KIT is now beside HERBERT upon the box, and so close to the Parkway wall that he can touch it. He looks at ARCHIE and MARY, who are still in each other's arm, with an expression of mixed wonder and resignation.*]

ARCHIE

You can't. I won't let you. Good-bye—good-bye—

> [*He holds her closer, kissing her tear-stained face. She keeps murmuring.*]

MARY

—A promise like that—and I can't save you—
can't save you—a promise like that—

[*But they take leave of each other.* KIT
watches them. His features set.]

KIT

[*To* HERBERT.]
I suppose this is what's called love.

HERBERT

Looks like it. [*He spits contemptuously over the
side of the cab.*] Nobody seems to enjoy it
much.

KIT

—Well, it's enough for me. —Tell your Aunt
Eunice her ponies won't help me—our horse deal is
off.

HERBERT

What's that?

[KIT *springs from the box over the wall, onto
the bench.* ARCHIE *and* MARY *are oblivious.*]

KIT

All off! —Here's where I turn philanthropist.
[*He turns and looks down over the wall at the horse.*]
Pull your nag's head up! [*He takes the pistol*

from his pocket and conceals it against his side.]
Hear me? Pull it up! Now grab the lines! Tight!
> [Mr. Inch *wanders in from Left wiping his
> brow. Mary and Archie hear nothing, see
> nothing. Slowly Kit raises the pistol and
> takes aim.*]

MR. INCH

Hey! Watch out there! That's loaded!

KIT

It's for a suffering horse—   [*With fine malice.*]
—the last god-damn suffering horse in the city.
> [Mary *leaves* Archie's *arms and stares in amaze-
> ment at* Kit.]

MR. INCH

Honest? Honest, is it?

HERBERT

It's true, Mr. Inch. Oh, stop 'im—quick—stop
'im!
> [Mr. Inch *drops his helmet behind the
> garbage-can, darts at* Kit *and snatches the
> pistol from his hand.*]

MR. INCH

Then let me!

KIT

Get out, you, or I'll— [*Suddenly he realizes* MR. INCH's *purpose and relinquishes the pistol.*] Go to it.

> [MR. INCH *takes trembling aim at the horse, but his wrist droops and his hand finally drops nervelessly to his side as he himself collapses upon the bench, murmuring:*]

MR. INCH

—Hadn't the guts. Just hadn't the guts.

> [*But in a swift movement* MARY *takes the pistol from him, goes to the wall and fires twice. After each shot a gong sounds. The horse is seen to rear up, and disappear again.* MAJOR INCH, *with a curious, long-drawn-out cry, very like a whinny, staggers on from Right, and pitches forward upon his face near the taxi-cab.* HERBERT *clambers down from his box, and out of view.*]

HERBERT'S VOICE

Josie! Josie!

> [ARCHIE, KIT *and* MR. INCH *hasten to the spot where the* MAJOR *lies.*]

KIT

It's the Major, all right.

HERBERT'S VOICE

[*From below.*]

Hold on a minute, Josie.   Herbert'll unhitch you.

MR. INCH

Oh dear, oh dear—

HERBERT'S VOICE

[*Joyfully.*]

He's still breathin'!   He's still breathin'!

[ARCHIE *and* MR. INCH *bend over the prostrate form of the* MAJOR.]

MR. INCH

Has—has any one a pocket-mirror?

MARY

Here—

[*She goes to them and gives* ARCHIE *a small mirror from her hand-bag.*]

MR. INCH

Ho-hold it in front of his mouth, Archie.

[ARCHIE *does so.*]

MARY

Poor old man.

[MAJOR INCH *sits up in the street, gazes into
the mirror, adjusts his necktie, strokes his
mustache and murmurs feebly.*]

MAJOR INCH

It was nothing.

HERBERT'S VOICE

There, dearie— Why, you're nothin' but a
bag o' bones. I can lift you myself.

MAJOR INCH

[*Barely audibly.*]
Ernest—

MR. INCH

Yes, Father?

MAJOR INCH

There is—still work to be done.
[MR. INCH *gulps.*]

MR. INCH

Yes, Father.
[*The* MAJOR *slumps back into* ARCHIE'S *arms.*
MR. INCH *clears his throat and begins
to sing in a quavering voice:*]

MR. INCH

"White Wings, they never grow weary—" [*A peaceful smile settles upon the* MAJOR's *countenance.*] "They carry me tenderly over the sea—" [*From Right,* HERBERT *enters, dragging his cab behind him. Upon the back seat of the cab, in a semi-recumbent posture, sits* JOSEPH, *the dying horse, with a large handkerchief bound about his brow.* HERBERT *is singing dolefully; one measure behind* MR. INCH.]

HERBERT

"White Wings they never grow weary. They carry me cheerily over the sea—"

MR. INCH

[*Simultaneously.*]

"Night comes, I long for my dearie—" [HERBERT *halts just behind the taxi-cab and mounts the seat beside* JOSEPH.] "I spread out my White Wings and fly home to thee." [HERBERT *feels for* JOSEPH's *heart-beat, then suddenly cries out:*]

HERBERT

He's gone! Oh me, poor Josie—he's gone!

[ARCHIE *and* MR. INCH *abruptly stop singing,* MARY *gazes intently at* HERBERT *and* JOSEPH, *then slowly and apprehensively turns to look at the* MAJOR.]

MARY

—And the Major's gone with him, Archie.

[ARCHIE *and* MR. INCH *stare incredulously at
the still face of the* MAJOR. *Then* ARCHIE
lifts the body by the shoulders.]

MR. INCH

Now we can take him home.

[*He takes the* MAJOR'S *feet, and he and* ARCHIE
lift him from the ground. KIT *starts the
taxi-cab, and backs it nearer to them.*]

ARCHIE

Oh, no—not in that.

MR. INCH

He'd never forgive us.

HERBERT

There was a horse.

[*A motor-truck is heard approaching from off
Right in the Boulevard, and above it. The
voice of the* CITY EMPLOYEE *calling lustily*]:

THE CITY EMPLOYEE

Sloppo! Sloppo!

[ARCHIE *indicates the cab, with his head.*]

ARCHIE

Here, Father—

[*As he and his father carry the* MAJOR's *body
Right to the cab, a heavy garbage-truck, par-
tially loaded, backs in Left in the Boulevard
and stops at the base of the Parkway steps.
Upon the driver's seat is the* CITY EMPLOYEE,
*a robust individual with a dirty face and a
decided manner. He interrupts his song,
and stares in wonder over the wall at the
group on the Parkway. With the assistance
of* KIT, *the* MAJOR *is propped up on the cab
seat beside* JOSEPH. KIT *has found a rope in
the taxi, and he and* MARY *begin to tie the
shafts of the horse-cab to the rear axle of the
taxi-cab.* HERBERT *is crooning sadly:*]

HERBERT

—Poor Josie—poor Josie— Where'll I lay my
Josie—where'll I lay 'im to rest?

KIT

Archie— [ARCHIE *turns to him. He nods in the
direction of* MARY.] *I'll* tie it.

[ARCHIE *goes to* MARY. *She takes his hand and
leads him to the taxi-cab.*]

MARY

Come, dear— I'll show you how—

[ARCHIE *mounts the driver's seat and takes the wheel.* MARY *stands on the running-board beside him.*]

MR. INCH

My hat—where's my hat?
[*He begins to search for it.* KIT *finishes hitching the taxi-cab to the horse-cab.*]

MARY

[*To* ARCHIE.]
Push that out with your foot. [ARCHIE *throws out the clutch.*] Now pull this in. There! [ARCHIE *sets the gears.*]

MR. INCH

My hat! I can't go without my hat! Has anybody seen my hat?

MARY

Now let go with your foot—very gently— [ARCHIE *releases the clutch and the taxi starts forward, very slowly.*] That's it!

ARCHIE

I like the feel of it.

MARY

Do you, Archie?

[*The procession begins to move slowly off Left.*
ARCHIE *is at the wheel,* MARY *beside him.*
MAJOR INCH *and* JOSEPH *sit silent and stiff
side by side on the seat of the open cab.*
HERBERT *marches on foot behind them, wip-
ing his eyes.* KIT *lights a cigarette and casually follows.*]

MR. INCH

Wait a minute! —My hat!
[*He looks under the bench.* HERBERT *begins
to sing, slowly and mournfully.*]

HERBERT

"Wiiite Wingssss, they nevurrr grow wee-ery.
They carrrry mee cherrilee ovurrr thee seeeee—"
[*The procession goes out, Left.* MR. INCH
*finds his hat behind the garbage-can and claps
it on his head.*]

HERBERT

[*Off Left.*]
"Night comes, I long forrr my dee-reeee, I sprread
out my Wiiite Wingsss, an' fly 'ome to theeeee—"

MR. INCH

Wait! Wait! Here I come! Here I come!

[HERBERT *has recommenced his dirge, which* *continues, in diminishing volume, throughout* *the following scene, to the final curtain.*]

THE CITY EMPLOYEE

Hey, you—! [MR. INCH *turns to him.*] —My buddy's sick.

MR. INCH

I—I'm sorry. Nausea?
[THE CITY EMPLOYEE *indicates the galvanized* *can, Right.*]

THE CITY EMPLOYEE

They give me orders to grab on to one o' you White Wings. Heave me that can o' dainties, will yuh? [MR. INCH *glances furtively at the can, then* *off Left, hesitates, and begins to bite his nails.*] What's a matter? Too good for it?

MR. INCH

I—I didn't say that.

THE CITY EMPLOYEE

C'mon, heave!
[MR. INCH *bears the can to the wall.*]

MR. INCH

I—I'm not employed f-for this sort of work.

THE CITY EMPLOYEE

Get under it!

[*With difficulty* MR. INCH *hands the can up
to him.*]

MR. INCH

I—I'll report you! I'll—

THE CITY EMPLOYEE

Don't let it throw you! [*He takes the can, dumps
it and hands it back.*] Throw it away!— Now
hop aboard an' we'll finish the rounds.

MR. INCH

I—I can't, I've got an engagement.

[*The man's huge hand shoots out and grasps
him by the collar.*]

THE CITY EMPLOYEE

—Not to-day, you ain't. [*He drags* MR. INCH
*over the wall onto the driver's seat, and grinds in the
gears of the truck.*] We'll see how yuh do. Maybe
getcha job permanent. [MR. INCH, *his face contorted, looks over his shoulder, Left, from whence
come the last dying strains of* HERBERT'S *song.*
THE CITY EMPLOYEE *again begins his own call.*]
Slopppoooo-o! Slopppooo-o! [*The truck begins to
move off Right.* MR. INCH *receives a sharp nudge*

in the side.]   Hey, you! Sing out! [MR. INCH
*lifts up his poor, suffering little face and bravely
sings out.*]

MR. INCH

Straw-berries!   Straw-*berries!*   Nice—fresh—
straw-*berries!*

CURTAIN